# THE LAW OF ALLOTMENTS

## AND ALLOTMENT GARDENS

### (ENGLAND AND WALES)

With Rules and Regulations of the Ministry of Agriculture and Fisheries, together with the Provisions, so far as they relate to Allotments and Allotment Gardens, of the Small Holdings and Allotments Act, 1908, the Land Settlement (Facilities) Act, 1919, the Acquisition of Land (Assessment of Compensation) Act, 1919, the Agriculture Act, 1920, and the Allotments Act, 1922

BY

## E. LAWRENCE MITCHELL

**Principal, Small Holdings and Allotments Branch of the Ministry of Agriculture and Fisheries.**

# CONTENTS.

| CHAP. | | PAGE |
|---|---|---|
| | INTRODUCTION . . . . . . . | vii |
| I | DEFINITION OF ALLOTMENT, ALLOTMENT GARDEN, ETC. . . . . . . . . | 1 |
| II | ALLOTMENTS PROVIDED UNDER THE ALLOTMENTS ACTS, 1908 TO 1922. . . . . . | 3 |
| III | ACQUISITION OF LAND BY ALLOTMENT AUTHORITIES | 14 |
| IV | FINANCE OF ALLOTMENT AUTHORITIES . . . | 34 |
| V | TENURE OF ALLOTMENTS AND ALLOTMENT GARDENS | 38 |
| VI | COMPENSATION PAYABLE ON DETERMINATION OF TENANCIES . . . . . . . | 44 |
| VII | RATING OF ALLOTMENTS . . . . . | 52 |
| VIII | GENERAL . . . . . . . . | 56 |

APPENDIX.

| | | |
|---|---|---|
| 1 | The Small Holdings and Allotments Act, 1908 . | 59 |
| 2 | The Land Settlement (Facilities) Act, 1919 . | 83 |
| 3 | The Allotments Act, 1922 . . . . . | 93 |
| 4 | The Acquisition of Land (Assessment of Compensation) Act, 1919 . . . . . . | 107 |
| 5 | The Agriculture Act, 1920 . . . . | 114 |
| 6 | The Small Holdings and Allotments (Compulsory Purchase) Regulations, 1922 . . | 120 |
| 7 | The Small Holdings and Allotments (Compulsory Hiring) Regulations, 1922 . . . . | 124 |
| 8 | Model Rules as to Allotment Gardens . . | 134 |
| 9 | Model Rules to be adopted by Co-operative Associations . . . . . . . . | 139 |
| 10 | Schedule of terms allowed by Ministry of Health for repayment of Loans for adaptation of Allotments | 140 |

# INTRODUCTION.

Until the passing of the Allotments Act, 1922, which received the Royal Assent on the 4th August of that year, the Acts appertaining to allotments had dealt almost entirely with the provision of allotments by local authorities and the compensation payable to tenants of allotments on the determination of their tenancies. The Act of 1922 contains provisions, however, restricting the power of landlords, who have let land for cultivation as allotment gardens, to terminate the tenancies which they have created and also entrusts to local authorities similar powers of entry on land which were obtained by the Board of Agriculture and Fisheries under the Defence of the Realm Regulations during the war. When it is realized that according to the latest official returns available (31st December, 1920) there were 1,330,000 allotment holders in England and Wales, of which approximately 500,000 were tenants of private owners, it will be seen that the Act of 1922 affects the rights of a large number of landowners, and has a much wider application than had previous allotment legislation. The growth of, and the demand for allotments in the vicinity of the cities and towns has made the question of the provision of land for the purpose one of vital importance to urban landowners, especially as their control over their property is to some extent restricted. The Act of 1922 is based apparently on the contention that this interference with private interests is justified by the national importance of providing garden plots for the dwellers in urban districts, and it is obvious that a knowledge of the statutes governing the tenure of land let as allotments or allotment gardens is necessary to the management of urban property which is awaiting development for building, etc.

The object of this textbook is to set out concisely the duties and powers of local authorities with regard to the provision of allotments and allotment gardens under the Allotments Acts, 1908 to 1922, and to explain the statutory provisions governing the tenure of allotments and allotment gardens generally and the rights of tenants to compensation on dispossession. The Acts dealing mainly with the matter are :—

(1) The Small Holdings and Allotments Act, 1908, referred to throughout as "the Act of 1908."
(2) The Land Settlement (Facilities) Act, 1919, referred to as "the Act of 1919."
(3) The Allotments Act, 1922, referred to as "the Act of 1922."

The provisions of the Acts of 1908 and 1919 which relate to allotments and the provisions of the Act of 1922 are to be cited together as the Allotments Acts, 1908 to 1922, and are referred to in this textbook as "the Acts."

A large number of allotments were provided during the war by local authorities acting as agents to the Board (now the Minister) of Agriculture and Fisheries in the exercise of powers contained in Regulations 2L and 2M of the Defence of the Realm Regulations. The Minister has, however, announced his decision to withdraw from possession of all such allotments not later than the 25th March, 1923, and these allotments will therefore cease to exist as such very shortly, although the local authorities have power to "re-acquire" such land under the Allotments Acts. For the sake of convenience it has not, therefore, been thought necessary to refer in detail to the powers under which these allotments were provided, or to the powers given under the various Public Inclosure Acts which required, in certain cases upon inclosures, the appropriation of allotments for the labouring poor, as these latter powers are only of very limited application.

Allotments and allotment gardens may be divided into two main classes :—

(a) Those provided by local authorities acting under the powers contained in the Allotments Acts, 1908 to 1922;
(b) Those provided by statutory companies and private landowners and let direct to individuals or allotment associations without any intervention on the part of a local authority.

As will be explained later, however, the provisions of

the Acts differ considerably in their application to allotments and allotment gardens respectively, *but where the context permits, the term " allotment" whenever used in this textbook includes " an allotment garden."*

The powers previously conferred on the Board of Agriculture and Fisheries are now vested in the Minister of Agriculture and Fisheries, who is legally the successor to the Board, but to avoid the personal note which is not practically applicable the term " the Ministry " is used throughout this textbook as referring to the Ministry of Agriculture and Fisheries.

# THE LAW OF ALLOTMENTS.

## CHAPTER I.

### DEFINITION OF ALLOTMENT AND ALLOTMENT GARDEN, ETC.

Until the Act of 1922 was passed the expressions "allotment" and "allotment garden" were not defined in specific terms in any of the previous Acts except that the word "allotment" included a field garden (section 61 of the Act of 1908). The term "allotment garden" was used for the first time in section 11 of the Agriculture Act, 1920, but it was not defined in that Act, an apparent omission which has since been remedied by the Act of 1922.

Section 3 of the Act of 1922 contains provisions as to compensation payable to tenants of allotments, and re-enacts with modifications as to the determination and recovery of compensation, the provisions of the Allotments and Cottage Gardens (Compensation for Crops) Act, 1887, which is repealed by the Act of 1922. Section 3 defines an allotment for the purpose of that section as "any parcel of land whether attached to a cottage or not of not more than two acres in extent held by a tenant under a landlord and cultivated as a farm or a garden or partly as a garden and partly as a farm." Under section 27 (3) of the Act of 1908, however, a local allotments authority may let an allotment "not exceeding 5 acres" and section 47 (3) of the same Act puts the tenant of such an allotment up to 5 acres in the same position as regards compensation as a tenant of an allotment not exceeding 2 acres.

To sum up, an allotment can therefore be defined as any parcel of land whether attached to a cottage or not of not more than 2 acres in extent or, if provided by a local authority under the Allotments Acts, of not more than 5 acres in extent, held by a tenant under a landlord and cultivated as a farm or a garden or partly as a garden and partly as a farm.

An allotment garden is defined in section 22 of the Act of 1922 as meaning "an allotment not exceeding 40 poles in extent which is wholly or mainly cultivated by the occupier for the production of vegetables or fruit crops for consumption by himself or his family." From the wording of section 3 (1) of the Act of 1922, it is clear that the expression "allotment garden" does not, for all practical purposes, include any parcel of land attached to a cottage.

The distinction between an allotment and an allotment garden is most important, as the provisions of the Act of 1922 which altered the existing law as to determination of tenancies (section 1) and compensation on quitting (section 2) apply only to allotment gardens and not to allotments which are not allotment gardens.

Throughout the Acts the expression "landlord" means in relation to any land the person for the time being entitled to receive the rents and profits of the land, and the expression "borough" in the Act of 1922 includes a metropolitan borough.

## CHAPTER II.

## ALLOTMENTS PROVIDED UNDER THE ALLOTMENTS ACTS, 1908 TO 1922.

*Allotment Authorities.*—The local authorities responsible for the provision of allotments are as follows:—

In London the London County Council (section 36 of the Act of 1908 and section 22 (5) of the Act of 1922) and the Metropolitan Borough Councils (section 24 of the Act of 1919).

In urban districts the borough councils (including the councils of county boroughs) and the urban district councils (section 23 of the Act of 1908).

In rural areas the parish council (section 23 of the Act of 1908) or the parish meeting where there is no parish council (section 61 (4) of the Act of 1908).

*Statutory obligation of Allotment Authorities.*—The London County Council and the council of a borough or urban district having a population of ten thousand or upwards according to the published returns of the last census for the time being are under a statutory obligation to provide allotment gardens not exceeding 20 poles in extent (section 13 of the Act of 1922). Other allotment authorities are under a statutory obligation to provide allotments up to 1 acre in extent (section 23 (4) of the Act of 1908).

In the case of all allotment authorities they may, if they so desire, and have land available, let allotments of any area not exceeding 5 acres, but as county councils have power to provide small holdings of an area exceeding 1 acre it is very rarely the practice of allotment authorities under present conditions to provide allotments exceeding 1 acre. As regards urban authorities, it is obvious that, in future, the largest authorities will confine themselves to the provision of small allotment gardens.

*Allotment Committees.*—The council of every borough or urban district with a population, according to the published returns of the last census for the time being of ten thousand or upwards, are required by section 14 of the Act of 1922, unless exempted by the Minister of Agriculture and Fisheries, after consultation with the Minister of Health, to establish an allotments committee. This committee may be an existing committee of the council, or a sub-committee of an existing committee, and all matters relating to the exercise and performance by the council of their duties and powers under the Acts as respects the provision of allotment gardens must stand referred to such committee (except the power of raising a rate or borrowing money). Moreover, unless the matter is urgent, the council must receive and consider the report of the committee before exercising their powers which stand referred to the committee, to whom the council may delegate with or without restrictions, any of their powers with the exceptions already referred to. Section 14 of the Act of 1922 introduces, however, a new method of constituting the allotments committee in such a case. It must comprise persons *non-members of the council* experienced in the management and cultivation of allotment gardens and representative of the interests of occupiers of allotment gardens in the borough or district. This definition will enable persons who do not happen to be occupiers of allotment gardens (e.g. secretaries of allotment associations, etc.) to qualify as representative or co-opted members of an allotments committee. The persons to be represented may be occupiers of allotment gardens whether the gardens are provided by the local authority or by private owners direct. The number of the representative or co-opted members must not exceed one-third of the total number of the members of the committee, or be less than two or one-fifth of such total number whichever be the larger number. The representative members must be appointed by the council.

In the case of a county borough, the small holdings committee, set up under section 50 of the Act of 1908, may be appointed as their allotments committee provided it is constituted to comply with the requirements of the Act of 1922 as to representative or co-opted members.

The accounts of any receipts or payments by and to an allotments committee under delegated powers are to be regarded as accounts of the council and made up and audited accordingly (section 14 (3) of the Act of 1922).

As regards those boroughs having a population of less than ten thousand, the council may, by virtue of section 22 of the Municipal Corporations Act, 1882, appoint out of their own body an allotments committee if they consider it necessary and desirable. The council of an urban district, having a population of less than ten thousand, and a parish council may appoint an allotments committee consisting either wholly or partly of members of the council (section 56 of the Local Government Act 1894) and a parish meeting may appoint a committee (section 19 (3) of the same Act).

*Allotment Managers.*—The council of a borough, urban district or parish may from time to time appoint, and when appointed remove allotment managers of land acquired by the council for allotments. The allotment managers may consist either partly of members of the council and partly of other persons or wholly of other persons, but an allotment manager must be a person residing in the locality, and contributing to the rate out of which the allotment expenses of the council are paid. The allotment managers must act under the direction of the council, and may be empowered to do anything in relation to the management of the allotments which the council are authorized to do, and to incur expenses to such amount as the council authorize (section 29 of the Act of 1908). A parish meeting may appoint a committee to manage allotments (section 19 (3) of the Local Government Act, 1894). It will be observed that the powers of allotment managers are restricted as compared with allotment committees who would ordinarily deal with the acquisition of land as well as its management when acquired.

*For whom Allotments may be provided.*—All suitable persons of either sex are eligible provided they are resident in the administrative area of the allotment authority. The limitation in the Act of 1908 confining the provision of allotments to persons belonging to the labouring population was repealed by the Act of 1919. The effect of sections 23 (1) and 24 (1) of the Act of 1908 as amended by the Act of 1919 and read with section 27 (6) of the Act of 1908 is to impose on allotment authorities a statutory duty to provide allotments for co-operative allotment societies or associations so constituted that the division of profits among the members of the society or association is prohibited or restricted (see also page 12).

*To whom application should be made.*—Applicants in London should write to the Clerk of the London County Council, or to the Clerk of their Metropolitan Borough Council. Applicants in urban districts should communicate with the Clerk of the Urban District Council or the Town Clerk, as the case may be, and applicants in rural parishes should write to the Clerk of the Parish Council, or to the Chairman of the Parish Meeting, if there be no parish council.

*Acquisition of Land.*—This important matter is dealt with in a separate chapter, page 14.

*Rents of Allotments.*—Each allotments authority is required to carry on the whole of its allotments undertaking on a self-supporting basis (see also page 35), and subject to this the only statutory direction as to the rents to be charged is that the allotments are to be let at the full fair rent obtainable for their use as allotments (section 16 (3) of the Act of 1922). Not more than a quarter's rent (except where the yearly rent is 20s. or less) is payable in advance (*ibid.*).

*Conditions of Tenancy.*—The statutory provisions governing the tenure of allotments and allotment gardens in regard to length of notice to quit and compensation to tenants on quitting are explained in detail on pages 38-49. The other conditions as to cultivation, etc., are usually regulated by rules made by the local authority which require to be confirmed by the Ministry (section 28 (1) of the Act of 1908). The Model Rules issued by the Ministry are printed on page 134. Copies of the rules when made must be supplied to any inhabitant of the district or parish gratis on demand (section 28 (4) of the Act of 1908). An allotment must not be sub-let except with the consent of the local authority providing it (section 27 (4) of the Act of 1908 as amended by the Act of 1919).

*Cultivation of Allotments.*—Any kind of agricultural, horticultural or garden cultivation can be practised and any kind of live stock or crops can be kept or grown provided they are not prohibited by the council's rules. When the land is let to the tenant for use as an allotment

ALLOTMENTS UNDER THE ALLOTMENTS ACTS 7

garden, it must be wholly or mainly cultivated by him for the production of vegetable or fruit crops for consumption by himself or his family. It should be noted that the words " wholly or mainly " apparently qualify not only the " cultivation " but also the " consumption " of the crops, and a tenant is not precluded from disposing of a portion of the produce of the allotment garden. For the purpose of safeguarding themselves against a liability for excessive compensation to an allotment holder on quitting, a council may prohibit the execution of market garden improvements, but if any tenant feels aggrieved by such prohibition, he may appeal to the Ministry to vary or annul the prohibition, and the decision of the Ministry is final (section 47 (1) of the Act of 1908). The general question of compensation for crops, etc., is dealt with on pages 44–49.

*Stamp Duty on Agreements for Letting Allotments.*—Stamp duty is not payable on any lease or agreement for the letting of any allotment provided by a local authority under the Acts or on any duplicate or counterpart where the rent does not exceed 10s. per annum, and no premium is paid (section 21 (5) of the Act of 1919).

*Ascertaining the Demand.*—The local authorities must take into consideration any representations as to the provision of allotments made to them in writing by any six registered Parliamentary electors or ratepayers resident in the borough, urban district, or parish (section 23 (2) of the Act of 1908). Normally the demand for allotments is quickly and clearly indicated to the local authority by the residents themselves who desire plots to cultivate, but it is also the duty of the county councils to ascertain the extent to which there is a demand for allotments by any persons or co-operative associations in the several urban districts and rural parishes in their respective counties (section 24 (1) of the Act of 1908 as amended by the Act of 1919).

*Improvement and Adaptation of Land for Allotments.*—The local authority may carry out works of drainage and fencing, acquire approaches, make roads, footpaths, etc., as they think fit, and generally maintain the allotments in a proper condition (section 26 (1) of the Act of 1908).

*Letting.*—The Model Rules of the Ministry, printed on page 134, provide for the proper regulation of the letting of allotment gardens, and for preventing any undue preference in the letting (section 28 (1) of the Act of 1908).

*Letting of Allotments in Areas Exceeding Five Acres.*—Borough,* urban district, and parish councils may in special circumstances, with the consent of the county council, let as an allotment a part of the land acquired by them for allotments that exceeds 5 acres (section 27 (3) of the Act of 1908).

*Temporary Letting of an Allotment.*—If the local authority are unable to find allotment tenants for all the allotment land they have acquired they may let it temporarily on twelve months' notice to any person, for instance, a market gardener or farmer, who need not reside in the district or parish, at the best annual rent which can be obtained (section 27 (5) of the Act of 1908).

*Power of Appropriation of Land.*—A council of a borough urban district or parish may, in a case where no power of appropriation is otherwise provided, with the consent of the Ministry of Agriculture and Fisheries and the Ministry of Health, and subject to such conditions as to the repayment of any loan obtained for the purpose of the acquisition of land or otherwise as the latter Ministry may impose :—

(a) appropriate for the purpose of allotments any land held by the council for other purposes of the council ; or

(b) appropriate for other purposes of the council land acquired by the council for allotments.

This applies, in the county of London, to the council of the county and to any metropolitan borough council (section 22 of the Act of 1919).

This power may be used with advantage to allow the use as allotments of land acquired for purposes such as cemetery extensions, building of schools, houses, etc., where it is not required for the purpose for which it was acquired, but it would appear that the Act contemplates

---

* Any provisions of the Act of 1908 in regard to allotments which require the sanction of, submission to, or order of a county council, do not apply in the case of a county borough (section 37 of the Act of 1908). County boroughs are therefore independent of the county council's approval to any steps taken by them to provide common pasture, sell superfluous land, or let an allotment exceeding 5 acres.

the more or less permanent utilization of the land as allotments rather than a temporary user for a short period only.

*Power to Exchange Land for Small Holdings and Allotments.*—A county council may sell or let to a borough, urban district, or parish council for the purpose of allotments any land acquired by them for small holdings, and a borough, urban district, or parish council may sell or let to the county council for the purpose of small holdings any land acquired by them for allotments (section 45 of Act of 1908). This enables land acquired for allotments to be sold or let for small holdings, and *vice versa*, notwithstanding the general rule that a corporation acquiring land under the Lands Clauses Act for any purpose cannot use it or apply it for any other purpose.

*Sale of Superfluous or Unsuitable Land.*—Under section 32 of the Act of 1908 as amended by the Act of 1919, a borough,* urban district, or parish council with the sanction of the county council have a free hand in selling, letting, or exchanging land originally acquired for allotments which is not needed for the purpose, or in lieu of which some more suitable land is available.

*Purchase of Fruit Trees, Seeds, Plants, Fertilizers, and Implements, etc., by Local Authorities.*—If the Council of any borough, urban district, or parish is of opinion that facilities for the purchase of fruit trees, seeds, plants, fertilizers, or implements required for allotments cannot be obtained by the allotment holders from a co-operative society, the council can itself purchase these articles and may sell them to the allotment holders, or, in the case of implements, allow their use at a price or charge sufficient to cover the cost of purchase (section 21 (1) and (2) of the Act of 1919).

*Houses on Allotments.*—Under section 26 of the Act of 1908, councils may erect buildings and adapt existing buildings on allotments, except that one dwelling-house only may be erected on one allotment which for this purpose must not be less than 1 acre. It is, however, very improbable that an allotment authority will be prepared to undertake the responsibility of erecting houses on allotments without any financial assistance from the Exchequer, especially as they would have to charge rents sufficient to cover the cost.

* See footnote on page 8.

*Provision of Common Pasture.*—A council of a borough* urban district, or parish, can acquire land for common pasture by means of a scheme submitted to and approved by an order of the county council. The rents receivable for the land must cover all the expenses incurred by the council, and rules may be made by the council regulating the turning out of animals, etc. (section 34 of the Act of 1908, as amended by the Act of 1919). This provision is of course applicable as a general rule to rural parishes only.

*Provision of Grazing Rights.*—A council can acquire for the purpose of allotments rights of grazing and other similar rights over the land acquired, including stints or other alienable rights of grazing. The council can then make regulations for letting these rights (section 42 of the Act of 1908 as amended by the Act of 1919). "Stints" are rights of turning out a limited number of cattle.

*Use of School Rooms in connection with Allotments.*—Rooms in public elementary schools may be used free of charge with the consent of any two managers for the purpose of discussion on any question relating to allotments under the Acts (section 35 of the Act of 1908).

*Parish Meetings.*—Any references in this textbook to a parish council apply to the parish meeting in the case of a rural parish not having a parish council (see section 61 (4) of the Act of 1908 and section 22 of the Act of 1922).

*Powers and Duties of County Councils in regard to Allotments.*—The powers conferred on borough urban district and parish councils in regard to allotments may in London be exercised by the London County Council (section 36 of the Act of 1908 and section 22 (5) of the Act of 1922). Any references in this textbook to a borough urban district or parish council apply, therefore, to the London County Council where the context permits.

As regards their administrative area each county council are in effect the supreme allotments authority and responsible for the provision of land in its county for this purpose. It is the council's duty, as already explained, to ascertain the demand for allotments by individuals in the several boroughs, urban districts, and rural parishes in the county or would-be demand if

* See footnote on page 8.

suitable land were available. The duty of the council does not, however, stop there. The county council are empowered to act in default of and may provide allotments at the expense of the borough urban district or parish council (see section 24 of the Act of 1908).

A county council may also let land acquired or appropriated by the council for small holdings for cultivation as an allotment or to a local authority or to a properly constituted co-operative association, for the purpose of being sub-let for such use (section 15 of the Act of 1922). This power is additional to that contained in section 17 of the Act of 1919 which enables a county council to acquire land for the purpose of leasing it to a parish council in their county for the provision of allotments. The exercise of these powers by a county council requires the consent of the Ministry until the 31st March, 1926. The proviso to section 15 of the Act of 1922 expressly states that a council are not authorized to let any land hired by the council, or authorize the use of the land hired, in contravention of any term or condition of the contract of tenancy. If, therefore, a county council hire pasture land for small holdings subject to a condition that it shall not be broken up, they are not empowered to let the land in allotments inasmuch as the use of the land for such purpose would inevitably involve the breaking up of the pasture.

*Duties and Powers of the Ministry.*—The Ministry of Agriculture and Fisheries is charged with a general oversight of the work of the local allotment authorities (except in regard to finance, which is a matter for the Ministry of Health), and has power to act in default of such authorities.

If the Ministry of Agriculture is satisfied after holding a local inquiry that the London County Council, the council of any county borough or metropolitan borough have failed to satisfy, to the extent to which it is reasonably practicable having regard to the provisions of the Acts, the demand for allotment gardens, the Ministry may transfer to the Small Holdings Commissioners all or any of the powers of the council relating to the provision of allotment gardens (section 20 of the Act of 1922). Similar powers are given to the Ministry in the case of failure on the part of both the non-county borough, urban district or parish council and the county council (section 24 of the Act of 1908 as amended by the Act of 1919). So far as borrowing powers, accounts, etc., are concerned, the procedure applicable in all cases of action in default is laid down in section 24 of the Act of 1908. At the local inquiry which is a necessary precedent to default action by the Ministry, the allotments authority (and the county council where the allotment authority is a non-county borough, urban districts or parish council) have a statutory right to appear and to be heard.

*Allotment Associations.*—Councils are under a statutory obligation to provide allotments or allotment gardens for an association so constituted that the division of profits among the members of the association is prohibited or restricted (section 27 (6) of the Act of 1908). Land may be sold as well as let to such an association. The Ministry, whose consent is necessary to the sale or letting to an association, have issued rules which must be adopted by associations desiring to hire or buy land for allotments or allotment gardens from a local authority (see page 139).

Boroughs and urban districts are authorized to promote the formation and extension of co-operative allotment societies, and may employ as their agents for this purpose a Society having as its object or one of its objects the promotion of co-operation in connection with the cultivation of allotments (section 49 (1) and (4) of the Act of 1908). Borough and urban district councils may also, with the consent of the Ministry of Health, make grants or advances to co-operative allotment societies (section 49 (2) of the Act of 1908), and may borrow money for the purpose (section 53 of the Act of 1908 as amended by the Act of 1919). By these means allotment holders are enabled to organize themselves on a co-operative basis, and societies can be formed to assist them in the purchase of their requirements and in the sale of their surplus produce.

Any allotment holders or other persons who desire to form a co-operative allotment association should apply for advice and information either to the Agricultural Organization Society, 40 Broadway, Westminster, S.W.1, or to the National Union of Allotment Holders, 22 Buckingham Street, Strand, W.C.2. Both these bodies have issued approved model rules for co-operative allotment associations.

Societies or associations desiring to hold land must be registered under the Industrial and Provident Societies Act, 1893.

The Acts of 1908 and 1919 deal with the letting and selling of land by local authorities to associations of a distinct type and define precisely the character and constitution of such associations. Sections 1, 2, 11 and 17 of the Act of 1922 contain references to associations without the expression being defined. While it is true that the Act of 1922 is to be cited with the Acts of 1908 and 1919, there is nothing to indicate that the expression "association" in the above-mentioned sections of the Act of 1922 has the limited definition contained in the Act of 1908. In fact, sections 10 (1) (*a*) and 15 alone specially limit the definition of association in those sections, and it is submitted that the expression "association" in sections 1, 2, 11 and 17 of the Act of 1922 has a wider meaning and includes any association, however constituted, to which land has been let for the purpose of allotment gardens.

## CHAPTER III.

## ACQUISITION OF LAND BY ALLOTMENT AUTHORITIES

Councils can acquire land for the provision of allotments and allotment gardens in three different ways :—
 (i) by purchase or hiring by voluntary agreement ;
 (ii) compulsorily under an order for purchase or hiring ;
 (iii) by entry upon land.

Strictly speaking the procedure under (iii) is not acquisition, as the council merely enter on and occupy the land. This power can only be exercised for the purpose of providing allotment gardens.

*Acquisition by voluntary agreement.*—For the purpose of providing allotments borough, urban district or parish councils may by agreement purchase or take on lease land whether situate within or without their borough, district or parish (section 25 (1) of the Act of 1908).

The form of lease printed on page 18 is equally applicable to cases of voluntary hiring by a council with the omission of paragraph 8.

Under Section 40 (5) of the Small Holdings and Allotments Act, 1908, a person having the powers of a tenant for life within the meaning of the Settled Land Acts 1882–1890, may grant the settled land or part thereof to a county council for the purpose of small holdings in perpetuity at a fee or other rent secured by condition of re-entry or otherwise as may be agreed upon. Under section 9 of the Act of 1922 this power is extended to the acquisition of land by the council of a borough or urban district for the purpose of providing allotments, and the council may covenant to pay the fee farm or other rent. Any acquisition on this basis must be a voluntary arrangement between the council and the landowner.

In a case where a local authority have agreed with the

owner to acquire land for allotments and the land is let to a yearly tenant or a tenant from year to year, the council can at any time after such agreement give not less than fourteen days' notice to the tenant and can then enter on and take possession of the land subject to the payment of compensation to the tenant as if the council had used compulsory powers to acquire his interest (section 2 (2) and (4) of the Act of 1919). This enables councils to obtain early possession of land which may be let to a tenant whose tenancy could not be determined by notice to quit except after the expiration of a year or more.

*Compulsory acquisition under an order for purchase or hiring.*—If suitable land cannot be acquired by agreement on reasonable terms a parish council may represent the case to the county council, who may, on behalf of the parish council, exercise powers of compulsory acquisition (section 39 (7) of the Act of 1908). The borough and urban district councils are themselves empowered to acquire land compulsorily for allotments.

A county, borough, or urban district council may make an order for the compulsory acquisition for allotments of any land except—

(a) any park or home farm attached to and usually occupied with a mansion house if the land is required for the amenity or convenience of the mansion house;

(b) any garden or pleasure ground or any land required for the amenity or convenience of any dwelling-house;

(c) the whole or part of a holding of 50 acres or less in extent or of an annual value not exceeding £50 for the purpose of income tax, where it is shown to the satisfaction of the council that the holding is the principal means of livelihood of the occupier, except when the occupier is a tenant, and consents to the acquisition.*

---

* It has been thought desirable to include this paragraph under the heading of land in respect of which a council may not make a compulsory order. Strictly speaking, however, the effect of section 16 of the Act of 1919 is that a council may make an order (which will not until 31st December, 1922, require the Ministry's consent) in respect of such land, but they cannot carry the order into effect and acquire the land so long as the council are satisfied that the land is the principal means of livelihood of the tenant.

(d) land owned by a local authority, the site of an ancient monument, etc., and in certain circumstances, woodland. (Section 41 of the Act of 1908, as amended by section 16 of the Act of 1919.)

(e) any land which forms part of the trust property to which the National Trust Act, 1907, applies (section 28 (4) of the Act of 1919). The council of the National Trust hold, for the benefit of the nation, places of historic interest or natural beauty.

Further, as regards land which has been acquired by any Corporation or Company for the purposes of a railway, dock, canal, water or other public undertaking, compulsory acquisition can only proceed by way of a *hiring* order subject to a condition enabling the corporation or company to resume possession of the land when required by them for the purpose (not being the use of the land for agriculture) for which it was acquired by them (section 8 (2) of the Act of 1922).

Pasture land is also conditionally exempt from compulsory acquisition. No land can be *hired* compulsorily which at the date of the order is pasture land if it is proved to the satisfaction of the Ministry that arable land which is equally suitable for the purpose of allotments to the pasture land proposed to be hired is reasonably available for hiring by the council (section 8 (4) of the Act of 1922). It will be observed that the onus of proof that equally suitable arable land is reasonably available rests with the parties who object to the hiring of the pasture land by the council.

As regards commons and open spaces, a grant or inclosure of common purporting to be made under a compulsory order made by a council is not valid unless it is made with the consent of the Ministry under section 22 of the Commons Act, 1899. Any land which is or forms part of a metropolitan common or which is subject to regulation under an order or scheme made in pursuance of the Inclosure Acts, 1845 to 1899 or under any local, Act or otherwise or which is or forms part of any town or village green or of any area dedicated or appropriated as a public park, garden or pleasure ground or for use for the purposes of public recreation cannot be appropriated or acquired by a council for allotments except under the authority of an order for compulsory *purchase*. Any such order will require to be confirmed by the Ministry who are required to hold the same inquiries as are provided under the Commons Act, 1876, and the order if and when confirmed will be provisional only unless and until it is confirmed by Parliament. Any consent by the Ministry to the appropriation for allotments of part of a common other than of the kinds mentioned above must be laid before Parliament, and if a motion is carried in either House within twenty-one days dissenting from such appropriation the Ministry's order shall be cancelled (section 28 (1) and (2) of the Act of 1919).

Subject to the exceptions stated, land can be acquired compulsorily whether situate within or without the administrative area of the local authority making the order.

The first step is for the council to endeavour to acquire suitable land to satisfy any demand for allotments by negotiations with landowners and tenants. If the negotiations for voluntary acquisition fail, the council will have no alternative but to consider the exercise of their compulsory powers of acquisition. Having selected the land they will decide first whether to purchase or hire.

In this connection it may be observed that the powers of compulsory hiring have been specially framed and adapted to meet those cases where land has a present or prospective building value. These powers enable councils to obtain a perpetual tenancy of land at a fair rent without regard to any value which the land may possess for building, mining or other industrial purposes, but subject to the landlord's right of resumption when he requires the land in good faith for such purposes. Moreover the rent cannot be raised against the council in consequence of their own improvements.

After coming to a decision as to the making of an order, the council should first satisfy themselves that the land is not protected from compulsory acquisition (see above). This may in some cases prove a matter of some difficulty. For instance, no definition is given in the Acts of the expression "home farm." This is usually taken to mean a farm which is part of a large estate, but being attached to a mansion house is usually occupied with the mansion house. If such a farm were temporarily let it might still come within the definition of a home farm, but an ordinary farm comprising a farm-house in which the farmer resides is not a "home farm." Some difficulty may also be experienced in deciding whether land is required for the amenity or convenience of any dwellinghouse. Councils should, however, after careful consideration of all the circumstances, decide whether an order should be made, and in arriving at a decision should have regard to the area held or occupied in the locality by any owner or tenant, and should avoid, if possible, taking an undue or inconvenient quantity of land from any one owner or tenant.

If the order is for purchase the form should be as set out in the appendix to the Small Holdings and Allotments (Compulsory Purchase) Regulations, 1919 (see page 123). This form is quite straightforward, and should present no difficulties.

If the order is for hiring it should be remembered that land can only be hired compulsorily for a term of not less than 14 years nor more than 35 years (see 39 (2) of the Act of 1908), but the council may by giving the landlord not more than two years nor less than one year before the expiration of the tenancy notice in writing, renew the tenancy for such term, not being less than fourteen nor more than thirty-five years, as may be specified in the notice. In such case the rent for the period of renewal will, in default of agreement, be determined by an arbitrator under the Acquisition of Land (Assessment of Compensation) Act, 1919 (see later); but the other terms of the tenancy will remain as before (section 44 of the Act of 1908 and section 7 (2) of the Acquisition of Land (Assessment of Compensation) Act, 1919).

The schedule attached to the form of order for hiring must contain a form of lease. The lease contained in the schedule to the form of order appended has been drawn up by the Ministry and contains all necessary details, covenants, etc., although it may need amplification and amendment in some cases to conform to local customs or conditions.

### Form of Order for Compulsory Hiring.

1. The Mayor, Aldermen and Burgesses of the Borough of                   or the                   Urban District Council are hereby empowered to put in force as respects the land

described in the draft lease set forth in the schedule hereto the powers of compulsory hiring conferred by the Small Holdings and Allotments Acts, 1908 to 1919, and the Allotments Act, 1922, subject to the provisions of those Acts and to the Small Holdings and Allotments (Compulsory Hiring) Regulations, 1922, and to the terms of this Order.

2. The tenancy of the Council shall commence either on the [*twenty-fifth day of March*] or the [*twenty-ninth day of September*].\*

3. (*Where the land is glebe land or other land belonging to an ecclesiastical benefice insert the following paragraph.*) Any sum payable by way of compensation for the damage to be sustained by the owner by reason of severance or other injury affecting the land shall not be paid as directed by the Lands Clauses Acts, but shall be paid to the Ecclesiastical Commissioners to be applied by them as money paid to them upon a sale under the Ecclesiastical Leasing Acts of land belonging to a benefice.

4. The powers conferred by this Order shall cease after the expiration of three calendar months from the date hereof or from the date of confirmation by the Minister of Agriculture and Fisheries if the Order is so confirmed.†

(L.S.)          (Usual authentication.)
*Schedule.*

THIS INDENTURE made the            day of 19     BETWEEN            (hereinafter called "the lessor" which expression shall where the context so admits include his heirs executors administrators and assigns) of the one part and the Mayor, Aldermen and Burgesses of the Borough of           [or the Urban District Council of           ] (hereinafter called the "Corporation" [or "Council"] which expression shall where the context so admits include their successors and assigns and every person deriving title under them) of the other part, WITNESSETH that in consideration of the rent hereinafter reserved and the Covenants by the Corporation [Council] hereinafter contained the lessor doth hereby demise unto the Corporation [Council] ALL and singular the several pieces of land hereinafter more particularly described—except and always reserved unto the Lessor but subject to the rights of the Corporation [Council] hereinafter contained the right to take sell or carry away any

\* These dates shall be the half-yearly days customary in the district, but where the Order is made for the purpose of providing allotment gardens, the date of the commencement of the Council's tenancy shall not be a date between the 6th day of April and the 29th day of September. The year should not be inserted, but should be stated in the notice to treat.

† This means that notice to treat under the Order must be served within the period stated.

minerals gravel sand or clay, all mines minerals metals ores and other substrata whether of coal stone clay sand or any other metalliferous or mineral substance or produce whatsoever whether opened or unopened, worked or unworked within or under the said land (all of which are hereinafter collectively referred to as "the said mines and minerals") with full liberty and power for the persons entitled to the said mines and minerals at all times during the lease by underground workings only to win work and carry away the whole of the said mines and minerals and also to carry away the produce of any other mines nevertheless making reasonable compensation for any damage or subsidence which may be occasioned to any building on the said land by reason of such working and carrying away of the said mines and minerals as aforesaid or the exercise of the powers to be reserved as aforesaid such compensation to be settled by a single arbitrator in accordance with the Agricultural Holdings Acts, 1908 to 1920.

To HOLD the same for the term of          * years from the          † day of          † 19 † for the purpose of sub-letting the land for use by the tenants as allotment gardens under the Allotments Acts, 1908 to 1922. Yielding and paying therefore during the said term hereby granted unto the Lessor the rent of £          † to be paid without any deduction (except Landlord's Property Tax and Land Tax) on the last day of every current year of the said term.

AND the Corporation [Council] hereby covenant with the Lessor.

1. That the Corporation [Council] will during the continuance of the term hereby granted pay the said yearly rent at the times and in the manner at and in which the same is hereinbefore reserved and made payable without any deduction except as aforesaid.

2. And also will from time to time and at all times during the said term pay and discharge all rates and taxes which are now or may at any time hereinafter be assessed or charged upon the said demised land or the occupier in respect thereof the land tax (if any) and the Landlord's property tax alone excepted.

3. The Corporation [Council] shall at all times during the said term cultivate the said demised land in a proper manner.

4. The Corporation [Council] at the termination of the tenancy on quitting the said demised land shall be entitled to recover from the Lessor the compensation payable under Section two of the Allotments Act, 1922, and shall pay com-

---

\* The period of the lease must be inserted—being not less than 14 years and not more than 35 years.

† Omit these particulars.

ACQUISITION OF LAND BY ALLOTMENT AUTHORITIES 21

pensation for any depreciation of the said demised land by reason of any failure of the Corporation [Council] to observe the covenants on their part herein contained or by reason of any user of the land by the Corporation [Council].

5. The Corporation [Council] shall not without the consent of the Lessor fell or cut timber or trees or take sell or carry away any minerals gravel sand or clay except so far as may be necessary or convenient for the purpose of adapting the land for allotment gardens and except upon payment of compensation for minerals gravel sand or clay so used.

6. The Corporation [Council] will during the said term keep any buildings fences gates hedges and ditches on the said demised premises in good and substantial repair and condition.

7. Any question as to the amount of compensation payable to or by the Council under this Lease shall except where otherwise expressly provided, be determined in manner provided by the Allotments Act, 1922.

8. The notice required by Section 46 of the Small Holdings and Allotments Act, 1908, shall be a three months' notice.

IN WITNESS etc.

DESCRIPTION OF LAND.

| Parish | Nos. on Ordnance Survey Map | Description | Acreage |
| --- | --- | --- | --- |

The order having been made the next step is to issue the necessary notices, for which purpose the council must decide whether the order requires confirmation by the Ministry before it is valid. An order made before the 31st December, 1922, will not need to be confirmed by or receive the consent of the Ministry except in those cases where the land is subject to rights of common (see proviso to section 1 (1) and section 28 of the Act of 1919) or where the land forms part of a park or home farm (see section 16 of the Act of 1919). If the council are practially certain that :

(a) the order does not require confirmation, and
(b) the order is " good " (see point above with regard to land required for the amenity or convenience of a dwelling-house) ;

they might reasonably proceed to issue notices on the assumption that the order does not require confirmation and is otherwise valid, in which case objections to the order should not be invited.

This notice might be in the following form under

paragraph 2 of the Small Holdings and Allotments (Compulsory Hiring) Regulations, 1922.

[NOTICE OF MAKING OF AN ORDER for use in the case of Compulsory Acquisition by a Council where the Order does not require confirmation.]

### ALLOTMENTS ACTS, 1908–1922.

.......................................COUNCIL.

To....................................................

............................................

TAKE NOTICE that the.......................Council have made an Order for the Compulsory

(a) Hiring for a term of............years or
(b) Purchase..............................

of the land described in the Schedule hereto for the purpose of providing allotment gardens.

A copy of the Order (except any plan referred to therein) accompanies this Notice.

Upon application at ...................a copy of the plan to which reference is made in the Order may be obtained free of charge.

..................................
Town Clerk or
Clerk to the................Urban District Council.
..........................................
...............................................
............................19   .

SCHEDULE.

| Parish | Nos. on Ordnance Map. | Description | Acreage | Owner | Lessee and Occupier. |
|---|---|---|---|---|---|

If as a result of the service of a notice in the above form any point is raised by the owner that the land is part of a park or home farm, or is required for the amenity or convenience of a dwelling house, it would be desirable for the council to apply to the Ministry for confirmation of the order, as this would afford a means of obtaining a binding decision as to whether the order was valid, having regard to the terms of the latter part of section 39 (3) of the Act of 1908. For this purpose notices in the following form would have to be issued and steps taken to publish the order under paragraph 3 of the Small Holdings and Allotments (Compulsory Hiring) Regulations, 1922 (see page 125). Similar steps under paragraph 3 will, of course, have to be taken in any case in which the order requires confirmation.

> [NOTICE OF MAKING OF AN ORDER for use in the case of Compulsory Acquisition by a Council where the Order requires confirmation by the Minister of Agriculture and Fisheries.]
>
> *ALLOTMENTS ACTS,* 1908–1922.
>
> ....................................................COUNCIL.
> To........................................................
> ..........................................................
>
> TAKE NOTICE that the..........................................Council have made an Order for the Compulsory
>   (*a*) Purchase.............................or
>   (*b*) Hiring for a term of..............years
> of the land, described in the Schedule hereto for the purpose of providing allotment gardens.
> A copy of the Order accompanies this Notice.
> Upon application by any person interested in the land at .................................. copies of the Order (except the plan referred to therein) may be obtained free of charge and the plan to which reference is made in the Order may be inspected until the Order is submitted to the Ministry of Agriculture and Fisheries for confirmation.
> Every notice of objection to the Order or to the acquisition of these lands must be presented to the Ministry within a period of one calendar month from the *date on which this notice is sent.*
>
> ..................................
> Town Clerk; or
> Clerk to the...............Urban District Council.
> ..................................19
> Schedule.....................

DESCRIPTION OF LANDS.

As soon as the period of one month, during which objections may be signified, has expired the council should submit the order to the Ministry for confirmation. If objections have been received the Ministry arranges for a public local inquiry to be held, at which the Ministry's Commissioner or other officer appointed hears the council, all persons interested in the land and such other persons as he may think fit to allow. At the inquiry the clerk of the council who will ordinarily conduct the case for the council should be in a position, *inter alia,* to state that

24   THE LAW OF ALLOTMENTS

the council have been unable to acquire suitable land on reasonable terms, to show that an undue or inconvenient quantity of land will not under the order be taken from any one owner or tenant, to supply particulars of the unsatisfied demand for allotments, and to bring evidence as to the suitability for the purpose of the land proposed to be acquired. The Ministry then considers the report of the officer holding the inquiry and decides whether the order should be confirmed or not, and if confirmed, whether with or without modification.

After the order has been made and the prescribed notices of the making of the order have been given, or after confirmation, the next step is for the council to serve notices to treat on the parties interested in the land (see section 19 of the Lands Clauses Consolidation Act, 1845, and paragraph 6 of the Compulsory Hiring Regulations, page 126). Such a notice to treat in the case of compulsory hiring may be in the following form :—

THE ALLOTMENTS ACTS, 1908–1922, and ORDER made pursuant thereto on the          day of
  19    .

---

The                                   * (hereinafter called the Council / Corporation) hereby gives you notice that it requires to hire for a term of          * years commencing on the          day of     *† 19     and take for the purposes of providing allotments (or allotment gardens) under the provisions of the above-named Acts and of an order made thereunder on the          day of          * 19    , the land mentioned and described in the schedule hereto and delineated on the plan attached thereto and thereon coloured          which land the Council is by the said Order authorized to hire and take.

AND the Council hereby demands from you and from each and every one of you that particulars of your respective estates and interests in the said land and of the claims made by you and each and every one of you in respect thereof which particulars must be delivered to the undersigned the          at his office at          within 21 days after the service upon you of this notice.

AND the Council hereby gives you and each and every

  * These particulars should be inserted.
  † This date should be a date consistent with the Order on which the Council require their tenancy to commence.

## ACQUISITION OF LAND BY ALLOTMENT AUTHORITIES

of you further notice that it is willing to treat with you and with each and every of you for the hire of the said land for the purposes aforesaid and for which you or each or any of you may be entitled to be compensated under the said Act or the said Order.

AND the Council hereby gives you further notice that if for 21 days after the service hereof you or any of you respectively shall fail to state the particulars of your respective claims or shall not agree as to the amount of compensation and rent to be paid to you respectively by the Council in respect of the acquisition by the Council of the said land, the Council will require the amount of such compensation and rent to be settled in the manner provided by the said Acts and the Acquisition of Land (Assessment of Compensation) Act, 1919.

Dated this        day of        19 .

Town Clerk (or Clerk to the

Urban District Council).

Notice to treat under any compulsory order must be served by the council within three calendar months after the date of the order or where confirmation of the order is necessary, then after the date of confirmation, otherwise the order becomes null and void (section 12 (1) of the Act of 1922). Moreover where an order has so become null and void no further valid order can be made for a period of three years unless it is confirmed by the Ministry, who as a condition precedent to confirmation, must be satisfied that there are special reasons justifying the failure to exercise the powers under the original order and the making of the new order (section 12 (2) of the Act of 1922).

At the same time as the council serve notices to treat, or as soon as they receive particulars of claims from the interested parties, the council will wish to consider whether they should exercise the powers of early entry given to them by section 2 of the Act of 1919.

A council can at any time after they have served notice to treat give not less than fourteen days' notice to each owner, lessee and occupier, and can then enter on and take possession of the land leaving the amount of compensation (*i.e.*, the purchase price or annual rent, etc.), payable to the owner, lessee, or occupier, to be settled subsequently (sections 2 (1) and 2 (4) of the Act of 1919). A notice may apply either to the whole or to any part of the land included in the order which is specified in the notice (*ibid.*). If, however, the notice relates to land on which there is a dwelling-house, and the length of notice is less than three months, the occupier of the house may, within ten days of the service of the notice, appeal to arbitration against the notice, and in default of agreement, the arbitrator will be appointed by the President of the Surveyors' Institution (section 2 (3) of the Act of 1919). IT SHOULD BE NOTED, HOWEVER, THAT IF THE COUNCIL EXERCISE THEIR POWERS TO ENTER ON THE LAND UNDER SECTION 2 OF THE ACT OF 1919, THEY CANNOT SUBSEQUENTLY EXERCISE THEIR POWERS OF WITHDRAWAL UNDER SECTION 39 (8) OF THE ACT OF 1908, EXPLAINED LATER.

It is often a matter of great importance to enter at fourteen days' notice in order that the allotment holders may get on to the ground in time to prepare the land to enable them to get the advantage of the season's cropping, but councils would be well advised to take all possible steps to satisfy themselves that after taking into account the rents which will be receivable from the allotment holders and the price, rent, compensation, etc., likely to be awarded subsequently in default of agreement by the arbitrator, the council's allotments undertaking as a whole will be self-supporting.

A form of notice of entry which may be used in the case of compulsory hiring is as follows:—

NOTICE OF ENTRY UPON LAND IN RESPECT OF WHICH AN ORDER FOR THE COMPULSORY HIRING THEREOF HAS BEEN MADE.

WHEREAS under the provisions of the Allotments Acts, 1908–1922, and an Order made thereunder on the day of 19 , the were authorized compulsorily to hire from you the land mentioned and described in the Schedule to a Notice to Treat dated the day of 19 AND WHEREAS such notice to Treat was served upon you on the day of NOW THIS IS HEREBY TO GIVE YOU NOTICE that after the expiration of 14 days from the date hereof the will enter and take possession of the land specified in the Schedule to the Notice to Treat above mentioned.

GIVEN under my hand this day of 19 .
Town Clerk (or Clerk to the
Urban District Council).

ACQUISITION OF LAND BY ALLOTMENT AUTHORITIES 27

[Note. The forms of notice to treat and notice to enter can be adapted for use in cases of compulsory purchase.]

Failing agreement as to the compensation to be paid for land proposed to be purchased compulsorily and the amount of the rent, compensation, etc., in the case of land to be hired compulsorily, the matter will fall to be determined by arbitration under the Acquisition of Land (Assessment of Compensation) Act, 1919 (see page 107). This Act provides that the arbitrator shall be either—

(a) one of a panel of official arbitrators appointed under the Act;
(b) the Commissioners of Inland Revenue if the parties so agree;
(c) an arbitrator agreed upon between the parties.

The panel of official arbitrators has been appointed by the Reference Committee consisting of the Lord Chief Justice, the Master of the Rolls and the President of the Surveyors' Institution and the arbitrator to act in any particular case is selected by the Reference Committee. Up to date (Oct., 1922) this panel consists of two persons only, viz. Mr. Howard Martin, P.P.S.I., Lonsdale Chambers, 27 Chancery Lane, London, W.C.2., and Mr. John D. Wallis, Stanecliff, Disley, Cheshire.

Section 8 (3) of the Act of 1922 provides that notwithstanding anything contained in any other enactment counsel shall not be heard in any arbitration under the Allotments Acts unless the Ministry otherwise directs.

Forms of application for selection of an official arbitrator may be obtained from the Secretary to the Reference Committee, 121 Royal Courts of Justice, Strand, London, W.C.2. A fee of £1 is payable on every such application.

Attention is called to section 5 of the Acquisition of Land (Assessment of Compensation) Act, 1919, which provides that where the acquiring authority make an unconditional offer in writing of any sum as compensation to any claimant and the sum awarded by the arbitrator does not exceed the sum offered, the arbitrator shall, in the absence of special reasons, order the claimant to pay not only his own costs but also the costs of the acquiring authority incurred after the offer was made.

The scale of fees payable on awards of official arbitrators is as follows :—

A fee calculated by reference to the amount awarded to the claimant in accordance with the following scale :—

### Scale A.

| Amount awarded. | Amount of Fee. |
| --- | --- |
| Not exceeding £200 . . . | £5 5s. |
| Exceeding £200 but not exceeding £500 | £5 5s. with an addition of £1 1s. in respect of every £50 or part of £50 by which the amount awarded exceeds £200. |
| Exceeding £500 but not exceeding £1,000 | £11 1s. with an addition of £1 1s. in respect of every £100 or part of £100 by which the amount awarded exceeds £500. |
| Exceeding £1,000 . . . | £16 16s. with an addition of £1 1s. in respect of every £200 or part of £200 by which the amount awarded exceeds £1,000, but not exceeding in any case £105. |

In addition to the fees payable under the above scale, a further fee on the following scale is payable for each day or part of a day after the first day, where the hearing before the arbitrator in respect of any claim or matter referred to him occupies more than one day.

### Scale B.

| Amount Awarded. | Amount of Fee. |
| --- | --- |
|  | £ s. d. |
| Not exceeding £500 . . . . . . . . | 5 5 0 |
| Exceeding £500 and not exceeding £5,000 | 10 10 0 |
| Exceeding £5,000 and not exceeding £20,000 | 21 0 0 |
| Exceeding £20,000 . . . . . . . . | 42 0 0 |

For the purpose of the foregoing provision :—

Any time spent by the arbitrator in viewing any land which is the subject matter of the proceedings before him shall be treated as part of the hearing :

A day shall be taken to be a working period of five hours.

## ACQUISITION OF LAND BY ALLOTMENT AUTHORITIES

Where the award is in terms of rent or other annual payment, the following scales of fees marked A (2) and B (2) are substituted for the respective scales A and B set out above:—

### A. (2).

| Amount Awarded. | Amount of Fee. |
|---|---|
| Not exceeding £10 per annum | £5 5s. |
| Exceeding £10 per annum, but not exceeding £25 per annum. | £5 5s., with an addition of £1 1s. in respect of every £2 10s. or part of £2 10s. by which the rent, etc., awarded exceeds £10 per annum. |
| Exceeding £25 per annum, but not exceeding £50 per annum. | £11 11s., with an addition of £1 1s. in respect of every £5 or part of £5 by which the rent, etc., awarded exceeds £25 per annum. |
| Exceeding £50 per annum. | £16 16s., with an addition of £1 1s. in respect of every £10 or part of £10 by which the rent, etc., awarded exceeds £50 but not exceeding in any case £105. |

### B. (2).

| Amount awarded. | Amount of Fee. |
|---|---|
| Not exceeding £25 per annum . . . . | £5 5s. |
| Exceeding £25 per annum and not exceeding £250 per annum | £10 10s. |
| Exceeding £250 per annum and not exceeding £1,000 per annum | £21. |
| Exceeding £1,000 per annum . . . . | £42. |

[Note.—The fees prescribed in the above scales are in addition to the stamp duty changed on awards by the Stamp Act, 1891.]

In the case of land to be hired compulsorily for allotments the arbitrator is, under Part II. of the First Schedule to the Act of 1908, required to take into consideration the rent (if any) at which the land has been let, the annual value at which it is assessed for income tax or rating, the loss (if any) caused to the owner by severance, and the terms and conditions of the hiring, but he may not make any allowance in respect of any use to which the land might otherwise be put by the owner, being a use in respect of which the owner is entitled to resume possession.

If after the determination of the amount of the compensation (including, in the case of land hired compulsorily, the rent) to be paid to the landowner or other person, AND PROVIDED THE COUNCIL HAVE NOT EXERCISED THEIR POWERS TO ENTER ON THE LAND UNDER SECTION 2 OF THE LAND SETTLEMENT (FACILITIES) ACT 1919, it appears to the council that the land cannot be let for allotments, at such a rent as will secure the council from loss, the council may at any time within six weeks after the determination of the amount, withdraw any notice to treat served on any person, subject to the payment of compensation for any loss or expenses which he may have sustained or incurred, the amount of such compensation, in default of agreement, being determined by arbitration (section 39 (8) of the Act of 1908). This is a valuable provision which enables a local authority to withdraw if the amount of compensation (price or rent, etc.), fixed by an arbitrator is, in the council's opinion, too high; it enables them to get out of a bad bargain.

In a case of compulsory hiring, as soon as the compensation and rent have been determined, the owner is required on the council's application to execute a lease. If the owner refuses the council may execute the lease in duplicate, and forward a copy to the owner, a lease so executed having effect as if it had been executed by the owner. When the lease has been executed it will take effect from the specified date in the notice to treat and the council are entitled to enter on the land on that date. Paragraph 19 of the Compulsory Hiring Regulations explains the power of a council to enforce the right of entry.

Where land has been hired by a council compulsorily for allotments, and the land or any part thereof at any time during the council's tenancy is shown to the satisfaction of the Ministry to be required by the landlord for building, mining or other industrial purposes or for roads necessary therefor, the landlord may resume possession of the land or part thereof on giving twelve months' notice of his intention to do so, or such shorter notice as may be required by the order for the compulsory hiring of the land. If a part only of the land is resumed, the rent

## ACQUISITION OF LAND BY ALLOTMENT AUTHORITIES 31

payable by the council as from the date of resumption will be reduced by such sum as in default of agreement may be determined by an arbitrator under the Acquisition of Land (Assessment of Compensation) Act, 1919 (section 46 (1) of the Act of 1908 as amended by the Land Settlement (Facilities) Act of 1919).

In view of the provisions of section 1 of the Act of 1922 which enable an owner to re-enter on land let for use as allotment gardens after three months' notice in writing to the tenant under a power of re-entry contained in or affecting the contract of tenancy on account of the land being required for the above-mentioned purposes, it is to be expected that councils will arrange in the case of a lease entered into by them after the date of the passing of the Act of 1922 for the owner to resume possession in the case of compulsory hiring on three months' notice. Any compensation payable to the dispossessed plot-holders in such a case will be payable by the owner (see page 45).

On renewal of a compulsory hiring tenancy (see page 18) the landlord may claim a re-assessment of the rent, but the arbitrator is directed not to take into account any increase in the value of the land due to—
(a) improvements carried out by the council in respect of which they could claim compensation on quitting ;
(b) any use to which the land might be put, being a use in respect of which the landlord can resume possession, *e.g.* building, mining, or other industrial purpose ; or
(c) the establishment by the council of other allotments in the neighbourhood.

*Entry on unoccupied land.*—For the purpose of providing allotment gardens only (not allotments) a borough or urban district council or a county council acting in default of such authorities may under section 10 of the Act of 1922, after giving fourteen days' notice in writing to the owner, enter on unoccupied land. Unoccupied land is defined as meaning—
(a) land which at the date of the notice of intended entry is not the subject of a rateable occupation, *i.e.* involving liability to payment of the poor rate or any rate leviable in like manner ;
(b) land under D.O.R.A. allotments (see page vi.) at the date of intended entry provided the

land was not the subject of a rateable occupation when possession was first taken under the Defence of the Realm Regulations.

A council cannot enter on any land—
  (i) the property of a local authority or a public undertaking;
  (ii) any common, open space, public park and recreation ground;
  (iii) any part of the New Forest or of the trust property to which the National Trust Act, 1907, applies.

After entry the council may adapt the land and let it for use in the same manner as land acquired for allotment gardens under the council's powers already explained.

Any person who is interested in the land entered upon and who suffers loss thereby may claim compensation—
  (a) in the form of a lump sum for capital loss, etc.;
  (b) by way of periodical payments.

Any payment under (b) shall not exceed the rental value of the land which is defined as meaning the annual rent which a tenant might reasonably be expected to pay for the land if the land had continued in the same condition as at the date when entry was made under section 10 of the Act of 1922 or when possession was so first taken under the Defence of the Realm Regulations as the case may be.

The council may terminate their right of occupation by giving not less than six months' notice to the owner expiring on or before the 6th April or on or after the 29th September in any year. The council's right of occupation may also be determined by the owner giving not less than two months' notice to the council when the land is required for any purpose other than use for agriculture.

Notices given by the council to the owner are to be given in the same manner as is provided in paragraph 25 of the Compulsory Hiring Regulations page 131, and the expression "owner" is defined as including the person who, but for the occupation of the council, would be entitled to the possession of the land. The term therefore includes a lessee. This power of entry is analogous to the power taken by the Board of Agriculture and Fisheries during the War under the Defence of the Realm Regulations except that the power can now only be exercised in respect of "unoccupied" land. The basis of the compensation which may be claimed by the owner or other person interested in the land is on similar lines to that laid down in the Defence of the Realm (Acquisition of Land) Act, 1916, and it is to be expected that the power of entry will be mainly exercised, in the first instance, to enable possession of D.O.R.A. land at present under allotment gardens to be retained and thus avoid the dispossession of the plot-holders who are at present cultivating the land.

## CHAPTER IV.

## FINANCE OF ALLOTMENT AUTHORITIES.

*Borrowing Powers of Allotment Authorities.*—The financial authority in regard to allotments is the Ministry of Health.

Under section 53 (1) of the Act of 1908 all expenses incurred by the council of a borough, urban district or parish in relation to allotments must be defrayed—

(a) in the case of a borough or urban district council, as part of the general expenses of their execution of the Public Health Acts; and

(b) in the case of a parish council as part of the expenses of the council.

The council of a borough or urban district may borrow for the purpose of acquiring, improving, and adapting land for allotments, and of making grants and advances to a co-operative society in the same way as for the purposes of the Public Health Acts (section 53 (4) of the Act of 1908). Money so borrowed is not to be reckoned as part of the total debt of the council for the purpose of any enactment limiting the borrowing powers of the council (section 18 (2) of the Act of 1922).

A parish council may borrow for the purpose of the acquisition, improvement, and adaptation of land for allotments under and in accordance with the provisions of the Local Government Act, 1894, but the money so borrowed is not reckoned as part of the debt of the parish for the purpose of the limitation on borrowing under section 12 of that Act. (Section 53 (4) of the Act of 1908.)

Councils before borrowing must obtain the sanction of the Ministry of Health, and in addition a parish council must obtain the consent of the county council. They are then empowered to borrow in the open market or from the Public Works Loan Board, Old Jewry, London,

E.C.2. Under section 18 of the Act of 1922 the provisions of section 52 (2) of the Act of 1908 relating to loans by the Commissioners for small holdings purposes are extended to money borrowed by councils for the purpose of providing allotments. Under such provisions the loan is to be made at the minimum rate allowed for the time being for loans out of the local loans fund. At the present time (Oct. 1922) the rate charged is 5 per cent. The maximum period for the repayment of money borrowed for the purchase of land is by section 18 (1) of the Act of 1922 extended to 80 years, and in the case of any other purpose the maximum period is 50 years. As regards loans for the adaptation of land the period of the loan will depend on the term of the lease under which the council hold the land, if the same has been hired, and the probable duration and continuing utility of the works in respect of which the loan is required. A schedule showing the periods usually allowed by the Ministry of Health for the various kinds of adaptation work usually required in connection with allotments is printed on page 140.

*Limitation on Expenditure on Allotments and Rents to be Charged.*—The Act of 1922 lays down new principles as to the manner in which an allotment authority's undertaking should be carried on. Formerly a council were debarred from acquiring land save at such price or rent as would enable their expenses to be recouped out of the rents of the allotments. It was, therefore, necessary for a council when acquiring *fresh* land for allotments to obtain sufficient rents for the particular piece of land to cover all the expenses in respect of such land, even if the council's existing allotments showed a profit. The effect of section 16 of the Act of 1922 is that the whole of a council's allotments undertaking will now be treated as one unit and that the council must act on the principle that the undertaking is to be carried on upon a self-supporting basis. It is provided, however, that the expenses of the council for the purposes of section 16 shall not include—

> (a) expenses in relation to the acquisition of land other than the purchase price or rent or other compensation payable in respect of the land. These expenses include legal costs of investigating title and of the conveyance of land

purchased, legal costs in connection with the leasing of land, the costs incurred in any unsuccessful attempt to acquire land, and, in the case of compulsory acquisition, the costs incidental to any arbitration;
(b) expenses incurred in making roads to be used by the public;
(c) sinking fund charges in respect of loans raised in connection with the purchase of land. Section 22 (1) of the Act of 1922 defines "sinking fund charges" as including any charges for the repayment of loans whether by means of a sinking fund or otherwise.

On the expenditure side of a council's allotments undertaking must be included all expenses (except those set out above) in respect of land acquired for allotments whether acquired before or after the passing of the Act of 1922. These expenses would ordinarily be:—

(i) interest on any loans for the purchase of land or other compensation payable in respect of the acquisition of land.
(ii) rents payable by the council to owners of land.
(iii) expenses incurred in adapting the land, e.g. draining, fencing and dividing, making footpaths (i.e. interest and sinking fund charges in respect of any money borrowed for these purposes).
(iv) expenses incurred in maintaining drains, fences, approaches, etc.
(v) rates and taxes.
(vi) expenses of management, collection of rents, printing, stationery, etc.
(vii) compensation payable by the council to plotholders on the termination of their tenancies.

On the receipts side of the allotments undertaking will be entered the rents of the allotment holders and section 16 (4) of the Act of 1922 directs that land let by a council under the Allotment Acts for use as an allotment shall be let at the full fair rent for such use.

The future acquisition of land by a council will not, therefore, depend as in the past, on whether the estimated income from the particular piece of land proposed to be acquired covered the estimated outgoings, but on the financial position of the council's allotments undertaking as a whole, including the estimated receipts and expenditure in respect of the new land.

It will be observed that there is nothing in the Acts to prevent an allotments authority making a profit on their undertaking provided the rents charged to the plotholders are fixed in accordance with the statutory direction as to full fair rents.

*Recovery of Rent.*—Any rent of an allotment in arrear may be recovered by the council as landlords in the same manner as in any other case of landlord and tenant, viz. by distress, or action in the County Court (section 30 of the Act of 1908).

*Accounts.*—Separate accounts of receipts and expenditure are required to be kept by a council with respect to allotments (section 54 (1) of the Act of 1908), and an annual statement must be deposited in the borough, district, or parish for inspection by any ratepayer within one month after the end of the financial year, 31st March (section 54 (2) of the Act of 1908).

## CHAPTER V.

## TENURE OF ALLOTMENTS AND ALLOTMENT GARDENS.

*Determination of Tenancies.*—Until the passing of the Allotments Act, 1922, the tenure of allotments depended on the terms of the contract of tenancy except where the allotment having regard to its cultivation, etc., was a holding within the meaning of the Agricultural Holdings Act, 1908. The number of allotments which are agricultural holdings is, however, comparatively few, and the tenure of the large majority previously depended on the contract of tenancy. The Act of 1922 overrides the provisions of existing tenancies of land let for use as allotment gardens, and as the vast majority of allotments are allotment gardens, the provisions of section 1 of the Act are of great importance.

For the purpose of the section the term "allotment garden" bears the definition given on page 2 except that the section does not apply to any parcel of land attached to a cottage. The effect of the provisions is that a tenancy of land let for use by the tenant as an allotment garden or to any local authority or association for the purpose of being sub-let for use as allotment gardens cannot be terminated by the landlord except by—

(a) a six months' or longer notice to quit expiring on or before the sixth day of April, or on or after the twenty-ninth day of September in any year; or

(b) re-entry after three months' previous notice in writing under a power of re-entry contained in, or affecting the contract of tenancy on account of the land being required for building, mining, or any other industrial purpose, or for roads or sewers necessary in connection with any of those purposes;

(c) re-entry as above, in the case of land let by a railway dock, canal, water or other public undertaking on account of the land being required for the purpose for which it was acquired or held by the corporation or company not being the use of the land for agriculture.

(*Note.*—In case of emergency the corporation or company can re-enter by giving the notice (which may be less than three months) provided in the contract of tenancy).

The landlord can, however, re-enter for non-payment of rent or breach of any term or condition of the tenancy or on account of the tenant becoming bankrupt or compounding with his creditors or, where the tenant is an association, on account of its liquidation.

Where, under any contract of tenancy made before the passing of the Act, the tenancy is either by express provision or by implication made terminable by the landlord by notice to quit expiring on a date between the 6th day of April and the 29th day of September, the tenancy may be terminable by him on the 29th day of September.

If the tenancy of an allotment garden is terminated on the 29th day of September or the 11th day of October (i.e. Michaelmas or Old Michaelmas) or at any date between those dates, the tenant whose tenancy is so terminated shall be entitled at any time within twenty-one days after the termination of the tenancy to remove any crops growing on the land.

None of the foregoing provisions apply to land held by or on behalf of the Admiralty, War Department or Air Council when possession of the land is required for Naval, Military or Air Force purposes or to tenancies of Defence of the Realm allotment gardens. The provisions apply to other tenancies current at the date of the passing of the Act of 1922, but not so as to affect the operation of any notice to quit given or proceedings for recovery commenced before that date.

Where a local authority are themselves owners of the land let for use as allotment gardens, they may re-enter under a power in that behalf contained in or affecting the contract of tenancy in the case of land let by them, being land which was acquired by them under the Housing Acts, 1890–1921 before the passing of the Allotments Act, 1922, on account of the land being required by the council for the purposes of those Acts. The period of the notice to the tenants will depend on the contract of tenancy. In the case of other land let by a local authority they can re-enter under a power in that behalf contained in or affecting the contract of tenancy after three months' previous notice in writing to the tenant on account of the land being required by the local authority for the purpose (not being the use of the land for agriculture) for which it was acquired or appropriated by the council.

The position in regard to a tenant of a local authority on land *entered on* under section 10 of the Act of 1922, is, however, somewhat different. The tenancy created by the council in such a case terminates when the right of occupation of the council is terminated. This may occur in two ways—

(i) by not less than six months' notice by the council to the owner expiring on or before the 6th April or on or after the 29th September in any year.

(ii) by not less than two months' notice by the owner where the land is required for any purpose other than agriculture.

It is possible, therefore, that the tenant of an allotment garden provided by a council on land *entered on* under section 10 may have to vacate his plot on two months' or less notice from the council.

Such a tenant will have the same right to remove his crops as is explained above if his tenancy terminates on the 29th September or the 11th October or on any date between those dates.

For the purpose of all the above provisions the expression "industrial purpose" does not include use for agriculture or sport, and the expression "agriculture" includes forestry, horticulture and the keeping and breeding of live stock.

As regards allotments which do not come within the definition of allotment gardens or which are not agricultural holdings, the tenure depends on the terms of the contract of tenancy.

The tenure of the few allotments in the country which are holdings within the meaning of the Agricultural Holdings Acts is affected by the Agriculture Act, 1920.

The definition of "holding" in the Agricultural Holdings Act, 1908, is "any parcel of land held by a tenant which is either wholly agricultural or wholly pastoral or in part agricultural, and as to the residue pastoral or in whole or in part cultivated as a market garden and which is not let to the tenant during his continuance in any office appointment or employment held under the landlord." In the case of such a holding, section 28 of the Agriculture Act, 1920, provides that notwithstanding any provision in a contract of tenancy to the contrary a notice to quit is invalid if it purports to terminate the tenancy before the expiration of twelve months from the end of the then current year of tenancy. There are certain exceptions to this provision, e.g. when possession of this land is required (a) for naval, military or air force purposes, and (b) by a statutory company, government department, or local authority for the purpose other than agriculture for which it was acquired. Further exceptions are notices given in pursuance of a provision in the contract of tenancy for resumption for a purpose other than agriculture, and a notice given by a tenant to a sub-tenant.

*Determination of Questions Arising on Resumption of Land.*—As already explained a landlord can terminate the tenancy of an allotment garden by six months' or longer notice, expiring on or before the 6th April or on or after the 29th September. Apart from this power the tenancy of an allotment garden cannot in the case of a private landlord be terminated by notice to quit or re-entry except in the circumstances detailed on pages 38 and 39, and section 11 of the Act of 1922 renders it possible, in effect, for the owner's right to exercise such power of re-entry to be referred to arbitration.

The section provides that where land has been let to a local authority, or has been entered on by a local authority under section 10 for the purpose of being sub-let in allotment gardens and the landlord, or person who, but for the council's entry, would be entitled to possession of the land, proposes to resume possession, notice in writing of the purpose for which resumption is required must be given to the local authority who may, by a counter-notice served within ten days after the receipt of the notice on the person requiring possession, demand the question as to whether resumption of possession is required in good-faith, for the purpose specified in the notice shall be determined by arbitration under the Agricultural Holdings Act, 1908. Possession of the land cannot be resumed until the expiration of the said period of ten days or until the matter, if referred to arbitration, is determined. The section does not apply where resumption of possession is required by a corporation or company being the owners or lessees of a railway, dock, canal, water or other public undertaking, but with this exception it applies where land is let to a local authority or to an association, but not where land is let direct by a landlord to a private individual or individuals without the intervention of a local authority or association.

It will be observed that where a landlord has let land direct to individual tenants his plans for development will not be hampered by the possibility of, say, one tenant demanding that the good faith of the landlord's action in giving notice of re-entry should be referred to arbitration. Such reference can only take place on the demand of a local authority or association, who are tenants, and it is to be expected that such a body will not act unreasonably and without good grounds in exercising their powers in this matter. The fact that the arbitrator may in his discretion direct that the costs of the arbitration be paid by the local authority or association is, of course, an important factor. On the other hand it is apparently the intention of the section that a landlord should be deterred from giving notice of re-entry except when he, in good faith, requires possession for development.

The question of good faith may raise some difficulty, but it would appear that all that is required is for the owner to satisfy the arbitrator that in giving the notice, he (the owner) *bona fide* required possession of the land. Any question as to whether the owner could develop other land instead of the land let in allotment gardens, would not appear to be pertinent to the question before the arbitrator.

The provision will be applicable in the case of land let by a private landlord, who requires possession for building, mining or any other industrial purpose, or for roads or sewers in connection with any other of those purposes, and also in the case of land entered on by a local authority under section 10 of the Act of 1922,

## TENURE OF ALLOTMENTS AND ALLOTMENT GARDENS

where the owner as defined in that section requires the land for any purpose other than the use of land for agriculture.

Attention is drawn to the fact that the purposes for which an owner can resume possession of land *entered on* for allotment gardens are considerably wider than is the case where land is *let* by the owner for the purpose, either to a local authority, association or individual tenants. Moreover, in the former case, he can resume possession after two months' notice.

It should be noted that under section 22 (4) of the Act of 1922, where land is used by the tenant as an allotment garden, then for the purposes of the Act unless the contrary is proved the land shall be deemed to have been let to him to be used by him as an allotment garden, and similarly where land has been sub-let to him by a local authority or an association.

*Recovery of Possession of Allotments by an Allotments Authority.*—If the council desire to recover possession in the case of a notice to quit or failure to deliver up possession, they may under section of the Act of 1908 exercise one of the following remedies :—

(a) peaceable re-entry without process of law ;
(b) action in the County Court ;
(c) proceedings before justices under the Small Tenements Recovery Act, 1838.

*Rights of Tenant of an Allotment to Remove Fruit-trees, Fencing, etc., on Termination of Tenancy.*—A tenant of land let for use as an allotment, or as an allotment garden, may before the termination of the tenancy remove any fruit-trees or bushes provided and planted by the tenant, and any erection of fencing or other improvement erected or made by and at the expense of the tenant, making good any injury caused by such removal (section 4 (1) of the Act of 1922). Where a tenant of an allotment or an allotment garden has paid compensation to an outgoing tenant for any fruit-trees or bushes or other improvement, he is to have the same rights as to removal explained above as he would have had if the fruit-trees and bushes had been provided and planted, or the improvement had been made by him and at his expense (section 5 of the Act of 1922).

## CHAPTER VI.

## COMPENSATION PAYABLE ON DETERMINATION OF TENANCIES OF LAND USED FOR ALLOTMENTS AND ALLOTMENT GARDENS.

In considering the question of compensation it is necessary to divide allotments into two main classes :—
(1) Allotment gardens as defined on page 2.
(2) Allotments which do not come within such definition of allotment gardens.

*Allotment Gardens.*—No compensation for disturbance will in future be payable to tenants of allotment gardens, section 11 of the Agriculture Act, 1920, having been repealed by the Act of 1922. As regards compensation for crops, etc., section 2 of the Act of 1922 provides that compensation is recoverable by a tenant only if the tenancy is terminated by the landlord and is so terminated either—

(i) between the 6th day of April and the 29th day of September ; or
(ii) by re-entry at any time in the circumstances detailed in paragraphs (*b*) and (*c*) on pages 38 and 39.

No compensation will be payable on re-entry for non-payment of rent or breach of any term or condition of the tenancy or on account of the tenant's bankruptcy unless the tenancy is so terminated between the 6th April and the 29th September. Compensation is recoverable by a tenant whose tenancy is terminated by the termination of the tenancy of his landlord in the same way as if his tenancy had been terminated by notice to quit given by his landlord. This applies for example where a local authority or farmer sub-lets land for allotment gardens.

The compensation recoverable is for crops growing upon the land in the ordinary course of the cultivation

## COMPENSATION

of the land as an allotment garden, or allotment gardens, and for manure applied to the land. The basis of such compensation is the value thereof to an incoming tenant (section 22 (3) of the Act of 1922), and consequently only the unexhausted value of the manure applied will be taken into account. Any sum due to the landlord from the tenant in respect of rent or of any breach of the contract of tenancy, or wilful or negligent damage committed or permitted by the tenant, is to be taken into account in reduction of the compensation.

As regards any contract of tenancy made after the passing of the Act (i.e. after the 4th August, 1922) by which land is let to any local authority or association for the purpose of being sub-let for or by the tenants as allotment gardens, compensation will be payable by the landlord *notwithstanding any agreement to the contrary* and notwithstanding that the crops have been grown and the manure applied by the tenants of the local authority or association. It should be noted that section 23 of the Act of 1919 enabled landowners and local authorities or associations to agree in the contract of tenancy that no compensation should be payable by the landlord on the determination of the tenancy, but this section will no longer apply to land let to a local authority or association after the passing of the Act of 1922. Existing contracts made before the passing of the Act will not, however, be affected. The foregoing provisions do not apply to any tenancy terminated before the date of the passing of the Act or where a notice to quit has been given, re-entry made, or proceedings for recovery commenced before that date.

The tenant of an allotment garden provided by a local authority on land *entered on* under section 10 of the Act of 1922, whose tenancy is terminated by the termination of the right of occupation of the local authority, as explained on page 40, is entitled to recover from the authority the same compensation as would have been recoverable if his tenancy had been terminated by a notice to quit given by the authority. If therefore his tenancy is terminated between the 6th April and the 29th September in any year he will be entitled to compensation for crops and manure, unless he has agreed in his contract of tenancy with the local authority that the council shall not be liable to pay compensation. It is only as regards land *entered on* for allotment gardens under section 10 of the Act of 1922 that the liability for payment of compensation depends on the terms of the contract of tenancy between the allotment garden tenant and his landlord.

*Allotments.*—A tenant of an allotment, not being an allotment garden (see definition, page 1) on the termination of his tenancy by effluxion of time or for any other cause is under section 3 of the Act of 1922 entitled to compensation as follows :—

(a) for crops including fruit growing upon the land in the ordinary course of cultivation, and for labour expended upon and manure applied to the land ; and

(b) for fruit-trees or bushes provided and planted by the tenant with the previous consent in writing of the landlord, and for drains, outbuildings, pig-sties, fowl-houses or other structural improvements made or erected by and at the expense of the tenant on the land with such consent.

This compensation may be obtained from the landlord *notwithstanding any agreement to the contrary*, but any sum due to the landlord from the tenant in respect of rent or any breach of contract or wilful or negligent damage committed or permitted by the tenant, shall be taken into account in the reduction of the compensation.

If the allotment is a holding within the meaning of the Agricultural Holdings Act, 1908 (see definition on page 41), the tenant is entitled to compensation for disturbance under section 10 of the Agriculture Act, 1920, subject to the exceptions set out in that section which is printed on page 114.

The tenant of such an allotment may claim compensation for crops, etc., either under the Agricultural Holdings Acts or under the Allotments Act, 1922, but not under both.

While it is true that a tenant of an allotment not being an allotment garden can as an alternative claim compensation under the Agricultural Holdings Act, 1908, for the improvements set out in the first schedule to that Act, yet in the ordinary course he will naturally elect to claim under the Act of 1922, as under the Act of 1908

## COMPENSATION

an allotment tenant would only be able to claim, as a general rule, compensation for the application to the land of purchased artificial and other purchased manures, although in rural parishes where allotments sometimes run up to an area of 5 acres a tenant might have a claim for laying down land to temporary pasture and for residual manurial value as a result of stock being fed on the holding.

Under the Agricultural Holdings Act, 1908, as amended by the Agriculture Act, 1920, any claim for compensation for improvements under the former Act is, in the absence of agreement, determinable by an arbitrator appointed by the Ministry.

Under section 47 of the Small Holdings and Allotments Act, 1908, an allotment tenant under a local authority may claim compensation for the following:—

(1) planting of standard or other fruit-trees permanently set out;
(2) planting of fruit bushes permanently set out;
(3) planting of strawberry plants;
(4) planting of asparagus, rhubarb, and other vegetable crops which continue productive for two or more years;

unless the council have expressly prohibited in writing the execution of any such improvement. These improvements are usually described as "market gardening improvements," and the object of the provision allowing the council to prohibit the making of these improvements is to enable a council to protect themselves against heavy claims for compensation, but as a general rule, councils have in the past provided in their rules for an arrangement which allows a tenant to claim such compensation as fairly represents the increase in value of the holding to the council due to those improvements. It is the almost invariable practice of councils to "prohibit" the execution of these market gardening improvements.

A tenant of land let for use as an allotment or an allotment garden if holding under a contract of tenancy made with a mortgagor not binding on the mortgagee shall, on being deprived of possession by the mortgagee, be entitled to recover compensation from him as if he were the landlord and had terminated the tenancy, subject to the deduction from such compensation of any rent or other sum due from the tenant (section 4 (2) of the Act of 1922).

Where a tenant of an allotment or an allotment garden has paid compensation to an outgoing tenant for any fruit-trees or bushes or other improvement, he is to have the same rights as to compensation as he would have had if the fruit-trees or bushes had been provided and planted or the improvement had been made by him and at his expense (section 5 of the Act of 1922).

*Assessment and Recovery of Compensation.*—Under the Act of 1922 (section 6) the compensation recoverable under its provisions and such further compensation as is recoverable under the contract of tenancy is in future to be determined, in default of agreement, by a valuation made by a person appointed, if the parties cannot agree, by the Judge of the County Court having jurisdiction in the place where the land is situate. Application may be made in writing to the County Court Judge by the landlord or tenant, and if the compensation is not paid within 14 days after the amount of compensation is agreed or determined, it will be recoverable by order made by the County Court, as money ordered to be paid by a County Court under its ordinary jurisdiction is recoverable. The costs of the valuation will be recoverable from the landlord and the tenant in such proportion as the valuer directs and be recoverable from either of the parties.

Under section 22 of the Act of 1922 the designations of landlord and tenant shall continue to apply to the parties until the conclusion of any proceedings taken under the Act in respect of compensation and shall include the legal personal representative of either party.

None of the provisions explained above apply to tenants of allotments provided on land entered on under the Defence of the Realm Regulations or on land forming part of a Royal Park (section 7 of the Act of 1922). As explained on page vi. D.O.R.A. allotments as such will come to an end on or before the 25th March, 1923, while any land used as allotments in the Royal Parks will, it is understood, revert to its original use very shortly.

Where land has been hired by a council for allotments the council, *subject to any provision to the contrary in the agreement or order for compulsory hiring,* are entitled at the termination of the tenancy on quitting the land to compensation under the Agricultural Holdings Act, 1908, for any improvement mentioned in Part I of the Second Schedule of the Small Holdings and Allotments Act, 1908 (see page 82) and for any improvement mentioned in Part II of the Schedule which was necessary or proper to adapt the land for allotments, the consent of the landlord to such improvements not being necessary. In the case of land compulsorily hired, however, the amount of the compensation payable to the Council for these improvements is restricted to the sum which fairly represents the increase (if any) in the value to the landlord and his successors in title of the holding due to those improvements (section 47 (2) of the Act of 1908).

The table on the next page gives a general idea of the compensation payable to allotment holders.

## COMPENSATION TO ALLOTMENT HOLDERS (OTHER THAN D.O.R.A. ALLOTMENT HOLDERS).

| Description of Tenant. | Method by which his tenancy is terminated. | Compensation payable on the basis of value to an incoming tenant. |
|---|---|---|
| Tenant of an ordinary allotment garden. | 1. By a six months' or longer notice to quit expiring on or *before* the 6th April or on or *after* the 29th September. | Nil. |
| | 2. By a notice to quit given by the Admiralty War Department or Air Council where possession of the land is required for Naval, Military or Air Force purposes, expiring between the 6th April and the 29th September. | For crops growing upon the land in the ordinary course of cultivation as an allotment garden and for manure applied to the land. |
| | 3. By re-entry by the landlord on account of the land being required for building, mining or any other industrial purpose or by a local authority or by a railway dock, canal water or other public undertaking for the purpose (not being the use of the land for agriculture) for which it was acquired by the authority or company. | Ditto. |
| | 4. By re-entry by the landlord for non-payment of rent or breach of any term or condition of the tenancy or on account of the tenant becoming bankrupt— | |
| |   (*a*) if the tenancy is so terminated between the 6th April and 29th September. | Ditto. |
| |   (*b*) if the tenancy is so terminated between the 29th September and 6th April. | Nil. |
| Tenant of an allotment garden provided by a Local Authority on land entered on under section 10 of the Allotments Act, 1922. | 5. By the termination of the right of occupation of the Council— | |
| |   (*a*) between the 6th April and the 29th September in any year, and in the absence of any agreement between the Council and the tenant that no compensation shall be payable; | For crops growing upon the land in the ordinary course of cultivation as an allotment garden and for manure applied to the land. |
| |   (*b*) at any other date | Nil. |

## COMPENSATION PAYABLE

| | | |
|---|---|---|
| Tenant of an allotment (not being an allotment garden) not exceeding 2 acres if let by an ordinary landlord, and not exceeding 5 acres if let by a local authority under the Allotments Acts. | 6. By notice to quit on account of the land being required by a Government department, a local authority or by a railway, dock, canal, water, or other public undertaking for the purpose (not being the use of the land for agriculture) for which it was acquired by the department authority or company. | For crops including fruit growing upon the land in the ordinary course of cultivation and for labour expended upon and manure applied to the land or alternatively the amount which can be claimed under the Agricultural Holdings Acts, 1908 to 1920, custom or agreement, and in the case of an allotment let by a local authority the amount which can be claimed under section 47 of the Small Holdings and Allotments Act, 1908. |
| | 7. By effluxion of time (if the tenancy is for a term of less than 2 years certain) or any cause other than notice to quit. | Ditto. |
| | 8. By notice to quit given in any case other than that set out in 6 above—<br>(a) if it is an allotment to which the Agricultural Holdings Acts apply;*<br>(b) if it is not an allotment to which the Agricultural Holdings Acts apply. | Ditto.<br><br>For crops including fruit growing upon the land in the ordinary course of cultivation and for labour expended upon and manure applied to the land and in the case of an allotment let by a local authority the amount which can be claimed under section 47 of the Small Holdings and Allotments Act, 1908. |

* In addition the tenant will be entitled to compensation for disturbance (at least one year's rent and not more than two years' rent) under section 10 of the Agriculture Act, 1920.

## CHAPTER VII.

## RATING OF ALLOTMENTS.

Some confusion has arisen in the past as to the rating of land used for allotments. It has been alleged that rating authorities have not allowed the occupiers of allotments the benefits conferred on them by the Agricultural Rates Act, 1896, and the Allotments Rating Exemption Act, 1891. An explanatory leaflet on the subject has therefore been issued by the Ministry of Health and circulated to local authorities.

In giving a general explanation of the subject it will be convenient to deal with the matter under the headings of (1) the Poor Rate, (2) the General Rate in the Metropolis and (3) the General District Rates in Urban Districts.

1. *The Poor Rate.*—Allotments should be assessed to the poor rate on the same principles as other hereditaments, except that during the continuance of the Agricultural Rates Act, 1896, they are entitled, in the same way as agricultural land, to the partial exemption from rates mentioned below.

*Who may be rated.*—The occupier of every hereditament is ordinarily liable for payment of any poor rate assessed upon the hereditament, but in the case of allotments this general rule is modified by the following enactments:—

(a) Section 17 (1) of the Allotments Act, 1922, enacts that a council providing land for allotments whether under the Allotments Acts or otherwise may by notice to the rating authority require that the council shall be assessed to the rate as the occupiers of the land and in such case the council for the purposes of any subsequent rate levied by that authority are to be deemed to be the occupiers of the land.

(b) Under Subsection (2) of the same section the same provision may be applied to any association providing land for allotments if the rating authority agree.

(c) Section 109 of the Inclosure Act, 1845, and Section 13 (3) of the Allotments Extension Act, 1882, provide that where land is let in allotments under those Acts the allotment wardens, committee or trustees managing the allotments are for rating purposes to be deemed to be the occupiers.

(d) In addition to the foregoing provisions which relate exclusively to allotments reference may also be made to section 3 of the Poor Rate Assessment and Collection Act, 1869, which, as amended by the Increase of Rent and Mortgage Interest (Restrictions) Act, 1920, applies to all hereditaments of which the rateable value does not exceed £20 in the Metropolis, £16 5s. in Liverpool, £12 10s. in Manchester or Birmingham, or £10 if situated elsewhere. Under this section the overseers may agree with the owner of any hereditament to which the section applies that he will become liable for the rates whether the hereditament is occupied or not and to allow him a commission not exceeding 25 per cent on the amount of such rates.

*Basis of Assessment.*—The poor rate is based on the net annual or rateable value of the hereditament as shown in the valuation list in force at the time the rate is made. The net annual or rateable value of a hereditament is found by deducting from the gross estimated rental the probable average annual cost of the repairs, insurance and other expenses (if any) necessary to maintain the property in a state to command the estimated rental (Section 1, Parochial Assessment Act, 1836); and the "gross estimated rental" is defined by section 15 of the Union Assessment Committee Act, 1862, to be the rent at which the hereditament might reasonably be expected to let from year to year free of all usual tenant's rates and taxes and tithe rent charge if any.

*Objection against Assessment and Appeal against Rate.*—If any ratepayer is aggrieved at the amount at which he is assessed in the valuation list in force he may at any time make objection against that list before the Union

Assessment Committee; and if he fails to obtain from the Committee the relief he deems just he may then appeal to Special or Quarter Sessions against a poor rate based on that valuation list.

If the Union Assessment Committee, on objection made to them, reduce the rateable value of a hereditament the reduction will take effect as regards any poor rate current at the time when the objection was made and any subsequent poor rate based on that valuation list.

*Partial exemption of Allotments from Rates as Agricultural Land.*—The Agricultural Rates Act, 1896, provides that during the continuance of that Act the occupier of agricultural land (which is defined to include allotments) shall be liable in the case of every rate to which the Act applies to pay one half only of the rate in the pound payable in respect of buildings and other hereditaments. The Act applies to every local rate except (*a*) a rate which the occupier of agricultural land is liable, as compared with the occupier of buildings or other hereditaments to be assessed to or to pay in the proportion of one half or less than one half; or (*b*) a rate which is assessed under any commission of sewers or in respect of any drainage, wall, embankment or other work for the benefit of the land.

2. *The General Rate in the Metropolis.*—The General Rate in the Metropolis is to be assessed, made and levied as if it were the poor rate, and all enactments applying or referring to the poor rate are to be construed as applying or referring to the general rate (London Government Act, 1899, section 10 (2) ). Allotments in the Metropolis are accordingly assessed to the General Rate on their full rateable value, but the occupier is relieved from payment of half the amount of the rate by the Agricultural Rates Act, 1896.

There are special provisions in the Valuation (Metropolis) Act, 1869, as to objection against Valuation Lists in the Metropolis.

3. *General District Rates in Urban Districts.*—General District Rates in Urban Districts are levied on the occupier of all kinds of property for the time being assessable to the poor rate and are assessed on the full net annual value of such property, ascertained by the valuation list for the time being in force. In the case, however, of allotments and land used for certain other purposes the occupier of the land is to be assessed to the General Dis-

## RATING OF ALLOTMENTS

trict Rate in the proportion of one fourth part only of the net annual value (Section 211 (1) (b) Public Health Act, 1875; the Allotments Rating Exemption Act, 1891). The general district rate is therefore not a rate to which the Agricultural Rates Act, 1896, applies.

The provisions in the Allotments Act, 1922, the Inclosure Act, 1845, and the Allotments Extension Act, 1882, referred to above, with respect to the rating of the council or association providing the allotments or the wardens, committee or trustees managing the allotments apply to the general district rate equally with the poor rate.

In the case of the general district rate the Urban District Council have wider powers with respect to the rating of owners than those conferred by the Poor Rate Assessment and Collection Act, 1869, in the case of the poor rate. Under paragraph (1) (a) of section 211 of the Public Health Act, 1875, the owner instead of the occupier of the allotment may at the option of the urban authority be rated where the rateable value does not exceed £10, or where the land is let to weekly or monthly tenants, or where the rents become payable or are collected at any shorter period than quarterly. Where under this provision the owner is rated instead of the occupier he is to be assessed on such reduced estimate as the urban authority deem reasonable not being less than two thirds nor more than four fifths of the net annual value. In such cases the owner does not appear to be entitled also to the abatement provided by paragraph (b) of the subsection as extended by the Allotments Rating Exemption Act, 1891, since that paragraph refers in terms to the occupier of land used as allotments.

## CHAPTER VIII.

### GENERAL.

*Application of Allotments Acts to Crown Lands.*—Section 7 of the Act of 1922 provides that the provisions of the Act dealing with tenure and compensation in respect of allotments and allotment gardens shall apply to land vested in His Majesty in right of the Crown or the Duchy of Lancaster and to land forming part of the possessions of the Duchy of Cornwall.

*New Forest.*—Section 21 of the Act of 1922 contains provisions affecting those parts of the Forest now used for allotment gardens. The Commissioners of Woods are empowered to let for the purpose any land in the Forest which on the 5th April, 1922, was being used for the provision of allotment gardens and with the consent of the Ministry such further land not exceeding 60 acres as may be agreed between the Commissioners of Woods and the Verderers of the Forest.

*Agricultural Holdings Act, 1908, and the Agricultural Land Sales (Restriction of Notices to Quit) Act, 1919.*—Section 22 (6) of the Act of 1922 declares for the purpose of removing doubts that the expression " holding " in the above-mentioned Acts does not include any allotment garden or any land cultivated as a garden unless it is cultivated wholly or mainly for the purpose of the trade or business of market gardening.

*Damage to Allotment Gardens.*—Section 19 of the Act of 1922 provides that any person who by any act done without lawful authority or by negligence causes damage to any allotment garden or any crops or fences or buildings thereon shall be liable on summary conviction to a penalty not exceeding five pounds if notice of the provision is conspicuously displayed on or near the allotment garden.

The Ministry has suggested to allotment authorities that they should arrange to post the following notice on any land used for allotment gardens and that they should take proceedings against any person who does damage to the allotment garden or to crops, fences or buildings thereon by trespass or otherwise.

### NOTICE.

#### ALLOTMENTS ACT 1922.

This land is cultivated as allotment gardens. Any person who by any act done without lawful authority or by negligence causes damage to any crops, fences or buildings thereon is liable on summary conviction to a fine of £5.

The section above referred to applies however to all allotment gardens whether provided by a local authority or otherwise.

*Short Title of Acts.*—The provisions of the Small Holdings and Allotments Act, 1908, and the Land Settlement (Facilities) Act, 1919, which relate to allotments and the Allotments Act, 1922, may be cited together as the Allotments Acts, 1908 to 1922.

# APPENDIX.

## (I)

## THE SMALL HOLDINGS AND ALLOTMENTS ACT, 1908.

(8 EDW. 7, CH. 36),

as it is now to be read with the Land Settlement (Facilities) Act, 1919 (9 & 10 Geo. 5, Ch. 59), and the Allotments Act, 1922 (12 & 13 Geo. 5, Ch. 51) (so far as relates to allotments).

[Portions repealed are enclosed in square brackets. Other minor amendments are shown in bold type.]

PART I.

Be it enacted, etc. :—

2.—*Appointment of Small Holdings Commissioners, etc.* (1) With a view to extending the provision of small holdings, there shall continue to be Small Holdings Commissioners (herein-after referred to as "the Commissioners"), and the Board of Agriculture and Fisheries (herein-after referred to as "the Board") may appoint two or more persons possessed of a knowledge of agriculture to be Commissioners and may appoint such other officers for the purposes of this Act as the Board may, with the consent of the Treasury, determine.

3.—*Inquiries and Reports by Commissioners.* (4) If in the course of their inquiries the Commissioners receive any information as to the existence of a demand for allotments, they shall communicate the information to the councils of the county, and of the borough, urban district, or parish concerned.

9.—*Sale or Letting of Small Holdings.* (2) A county council shall have power—
    (a) to sell or to let one or more small holdings to a number of persons working on a co-operative system, provided such system be approved by the county council ; and
    (b) with the consent of the Board to let **or sell** one or more small holdings to any association formed for the

# APPENDIX

purposes of creating or promoting the creation of small holdings, and so constituted that the division of profits amongst the members of the association is prohibited or restricted.

## Part II.

23.—*Duty of Certain Councils to Provide Allotments.* (1) If the council of any borough, urban district, or parish are of opinion that there is a demand for allotments [for the labouring population] in the borough, urban district, or parish [and that such allotments cannot be obtained at a reasonable rent and on reasonable conditions by voluntary arrangement between the owners of land suitable for such allotments and the applicants for the same] the council shall provide a sufficient number of allotments, and shall let such allotments to persons [belonging to the labouring population] resident in the borough, district, or parish, and desiring to take the same.

(2) On a representation in writing to the council of any borough, urban district, or parish, by any six registered parliamentary electors or ratepayers resident in the borough, urban district, or parish, that the circumstances of the borough, urban district, or parish are such that it is the duty of the council to take proceedings under this Part of this Act therein, the council shall take such representation into consideration.

(3) (Repealed by the Act of 1919.)

(4) The duty of a council to provide allotments under this Act shall not include the duty of providing allotments exceeding one acre in extent.

24.—*Duty of County Councils to Act in Default of District and Parish Councils.* (1) It shall be the duty of a county council to ascertain the extent to which there is a demand for allotments by **any persons or by an association to which allotments may be let under this Act** in the several urban districts [other than boroughs] and rural parishes in the county, or would be a demand if suitable land were available, and the extent to which it is reasonably practicable, having regard to the provisions of this Act, to satisfy any such demand, and for that purpose to co-operate with such authorities, associations, and persons as they think best qualified to assist them, and take such other steps as they think necessary.

(2) The county council, if satisfied that the circumstances are such that land for allotments should be acquired by them under this section, shall pass a resolution to that effect, and thereupon the powers and duties of the district or parish **council** under the provisions of this Act relating to allotments

shall be transferred from that council to the county council, and the county council, in substitution for that council, shall proceed to acquire land in accordance with this Act, and otherwise execute this Act in the district or parish:

Provided that this section shall not affect the property in, or any powers or duties of the district or parish council in relation to, any land which before the passing of the resolution, was acquired by the district or parish council under this Act, or any enactment repealed by this Act.

(3) Where the powers of the district or parish council are, by virtue of this section, transferred to the county council, the following provisions shall have effect :—

(a) The provisions of this Act relating to allotments shall apply with the modifications necessary for giving effect to this section :

(b) The county council may borrow for the purposes of those provisions subject to the conditions, in the manner, and on the security of the rate, subject to, in, and on the security of which the district or parish council might have borrowed under those provisions. The council shall have power to charge the said rate with the repayment of the principal and interest of the loan, and the loan with the interest thereon shall be repaid by the district or parish council in like manner, and the charge shall have the like effect, as if the loan were lawfully raised and charged on that rate by the district or parish council.

(c) The county council shall keep separate accounts of all receipts and expenditure under this section :

(d) All sums received by the county council in respect of any land acquired under this section or the corresponding provision of any enactment repealed by this Act, otherwise than from any sale or exchange, in so far as they are not required for the payment of expenses incurred by them in respect of such land, shall be paid to the district or parish council :

(e) The county council may delegate to the district or parish council any powers under this Act relating to the management of the allotments, and the letting and use thereof, and the recovery of the rent and of possession thereof ; and, subject to the terms of the delegation, all expenses and receipts arising in the exercise of the powers so delegated shall be paid and dealt with as expenses and receipts of the district or parish council under this Act :

(f) The county council, on the request of the district or parish council, may, by order under their seal, transfer to that council all or any of the powers, duties, property, and liabilities vested in and imposed on the council by virtue of this section or the corresponding provision of any enactment repealed by this Act, as regards the district or parish, and the property so transferred shall be deemed to have been acquired by that council under this Act, and that council shall act accordingly.

(4) If the Board are, in relation to any urban district [other than a borough] or rural parish, satisfied, after holding a local inquiry at which the county council and the council of the district or parish, and such other persons as the person holding the inquiry may in his discretion think fit to allow, shall be permitted to appear and be heard, that the county council have failed to fulfil their obligations under this section, the Board may by order transfer to the Commissioners all or any of the powers of the county council under this section in relation to the district or parish, and this section shall apply as if references to the Commissioners were substituted for references to the county council and with such other adaptations as may be made by the order.

25.—*Acquisition of Land for Purpose of Act.* (1) The council of a borough, urban district, or parish may, for the purpose of providing allotments, by agreement, purchase or take on lease land, whether situate within or without their borough, district, or parish.

(2) If a council are unable to acquire by agreement, and on reasonable terms, suitable land for the purpose of allotments, they may acquire land compulsorily in accordance with the provisions of this Act relating to compulsory acquisition of land.

(3) (Repealed by the Act of 1922.)

26.—*Improvement and Adaptation of Land for Allotments.* (1) The council of a borough, urban district, or parish may improve any land acquired by them for allotments and adapt the same for letting in allotments, by draining, fencing, and dividing the same, acquiring approaches, making roads and otherwise, as they think fit, and may from time to time do such things as may be necessary for maintaining such drains, fences, approaches, and roads, or otherwise for maintaining the allotments in a proper condition.

(2) The council may also adapt the land for allotments by erecting buildings and making adaptations of existing buildings, but so that not more than one dwelling-house shall be erected for occupation with any one allotment; and no dwelling-house shall be erected for occupation with any allotment of less than one acre.

27.—*Provisions as to Letting of Allotments.* (1) (Repealed by the Act of 1922.)

## SMALL HOLDINGS AND ALLOTMENTS ACT, 1908

(2) (Repealed by the Act of 1919.)

(3) One person shall not hold any allotment or allotments acquired under this Part of this Act, or any enactment hereby repealed, exceeding five acres:

Provided that any part of the land acquired by a council for the purposes of allotments which exceeds five acres may be adapted for letting and let as an allotment, if the county council are satisfied by the council that it is convenient and desirable that it should be so let and consent to such letting accordingly.

(4) An allotment shall not be sublet **except with the consent of the council.**

(5) If at any time an allotment cannot be let in accordance with the provisions of this Act and the rules made thereunder, the same may be let to any person whatever at the best annual rent which can be obtained for the same, without any premium or fine, and on such terms as may enable possession thereof to be resumed within a period not exceeding twelve months if it should at any time be required to be let under the provisions aforesaid.

(6) A council shall have the same power of letting one or more allotments to persons working on a co-operative system or **of letting or selling** to an association formed for the purposes of creating or promoting the creation of allotments as may be exercised as respects small holdings by a county council.

28.—*Rules as to Letting Allotments.* (1) Subject to the provisions of this Act, a borough, urban district, or parish council may make such rules as appear to be necessary or proper for regulating the letting of allotments under this Act, and for preventing any undue preference in the letting thereof, and generally for carrying the provisions of this Part of this Act into effect.

(2) Rules under this section may define the persons eligible to be tenants of allotments, the notices to be given for the letting thereof, the size of the allotments, the conditions under which they are to be cultivated, and the rent to be paid for them.

(3) All such rules shall make provision for reasonable notice to be given to a tenant of any allotment of the determination of his tenancy.

Rules under this section shall not be of any force unless and until they have been confirmed by the Board in like manner and subject to the like provisions as in the case of byelaws required to be confirmed by the Local Government Board under the Public Health Acts.

(4) Rules for the time being in force under this section shall be binding on all persons whatsoever; and the council shall cause them to be from time to time made known, in

such manner as the council think fit, to all persons interested, and shall cause a copy thereof to be given gratis to any inhabitant of the district or parish demanding the same.

29.—*Management of Allotments.* (1) The council of a borough, urban district, or parish may from time to time appoint, and, when appointed, remove allotment managers of land acquired by the council for allotments, and the allotment managers shall consist either partly of members of the council and partly of other persons, or wholly of other persons, so that in either case such other persons be persons residing in the locality and contributing to the rate out of which the expenses of the council under this Act are paid.

(2) The proceedings and powers of allotment managers shall be such as, subject to the provisions of this Act, may be directed by the council; the allotment managers may be empowered by the council to do anything in relation to the management of the allotments which the council are authorized to do and to incur expenses to such amount as the council authorize, and any expenses properly so incurred shall be deemed to be expenses of the council under this Act.

30.—*Recovery of Rent and Possession of Allotments.* (1) The rent for an allotment let by a council in pursuance of this Act, and the possession of such an allotment in the case of any notice to quit, or failure to deliver up possession thereof as required by law, may be recovered by the council as landlords, in the like manner as in any other case of landlord and tenant.

(2) If the rent for any allotment is in arrear for not less than forty days, or if it appears to the council that the tenant of an allotment not less than three months after the commencement of the tenancy thereof has not duly observed the rules affecting the allotment made by or in pursuance of this Act, or is resident more than one mile out of the borough, district, or parish for which the allotments are provided, the council may serve upon the tenant, or, if he is residing out of the borough, district, or parish, leave at his last known place of abode in the borough, district, or parish, or fix in some conspicuous manner on the allotment, a written notice determining the tenancy at the expiration of one month after the notice has been so served or affixed, and thereupon the tenancy shall be determined accordingly:

(3) Upon the recovery of an allotment from any tenant, the court directing the recovery may stay delivery of possession until payment of the compensation (if any) due to the outgoing tenant has been made or secured to the satisfaction of the court.

31. (Repealed by the Act of 1919.)

32.—*Sale of Superfluous or Unsuitable Land.* (1) Where the council of any borough, urban district, or parish are of opinion that any land acquired by them for allotments or any part thereof is not needed for the purpose of allotments, or that some more suitable land is available, they may, with the sanction of the county council, sell or let such land otherwise than under the provisions of this Act, or exchange the land for other land more suitable for allotments, and may pay or receive money for equality of exchange.

(2) The proceeds of a sale under this Act of land acquired for allotments, and any money received by the council on any such exchange as aforesaid by way of equality of exchange, shall be applied in discharging, either by way of a sinking fund or otherwise, the debts and liabilities of the council in respect of the land acquired by the council for allotments, or in acquiring, adapting, and improving other land for allotments, and any surplus remaining may be applied for any purpose for which capital money may be applied, and which is approved by the Local Government Board ; and the interest thereon (if any) and any money received from the letting of the land may be applied in acquiring other land for allotments, or shall be applied in like manner as receipts from allotments under this Act are applicable.

(3) (Repealed by the Act of 1919.)

33.—*Transfer of Allotments to Borough, District, and Parish Councils.* (1) The allotment wardens under the Inclosure Acts, 1845 to 1882, having the management of any land appropriated under those Acts either before or after the passing of this Act for allotments or field gardens for the labouring poor of any place, may, by agreement with the council of the borough, urban district, or parish, within whose borough, district, or parish that place is wholly or partly situate, transfer the management of that land to the council, upon such terms and conditions as may be agreed upon with the sanction, as regards the allotment wardens, of the Board, and thereupon the land shall vest in the council.

(2) All trustees within the meaning of the Allotments Extension Act, 1882, required or authorized by that or any other Act to let lands in allotments to cottagers, labourers, journeymen, or others in any place, may, if they think fit, in lieu of letting the land in manner provided by the said Acts, sell or let the land to the council of the borough, urban district, or parish in which such place is wholly or partly situate, upon such terms as may be agreed upon, with the sanction, as regards the trustees, of the Charity Commissioners or the Board of Education, as the case may require.

(3) Where, as respects any rural parish, any Act constitutes any persons wardens of allotments, or authorizes or requires the appointment or election of any wardens, committee, or managers for the purpose of allotments, the powers and duties of the wardens, committee, or managers shall,

subject to the provisions of this Act, be exercised and performed by the parish council, or, in the case of a parish not having a parish council, by persons appointed by the parish meeting, and it shall not be necessary to make the said appointment or to hold the said election.

(4) The provisions of this Act relating to allotments shall apply to land vested in, or the management whereof has been transferred to, a council under this section or the corresponding provision of any enactment repealed by this Act in like manner as if the land had been acquired by the council under the general powers of this Part of this Act.

34.—*Power to Make Scheme for Provision of Common Pasture.* (1) Where it appears to the council of any borough, urban district, or parish that, as regards their borough, district, or parish, land can be acquired for affording common pasture at such price or rent that all expenses incurred by the council in acquiring the land and otherwise in relation to the land when acquired may reasonably be expected to be recouped out of the charges paid in respect thereof, and that the acquisition of such land is desirable in view of the wants and circumstances of the [labouring] population, the council may submit to the council of the county in which the borough, district, or parish is wholly or partly situate a scheme for providing such common pasture.

(2) The county council, if satisfied of the expediency of such scheme, may by order authorize the council which submitted it to carry it into effect, and, upon such an order being made, the provisions of this Act relating to allotments shall, with the necessary modifications, apply in like manner as if " allotments " in those provisions included common pasture, and " rent " included a charge for turning out an animal :

Providing that the rules made under those provisions may extend to regulating the turning out of animals on the common pasture, to defining the persons entitled to turn them out, the number to be turned out, and the conditions under which animals may be turned out, and fixing the charges to be made for each animal, and otherwise to regulating the common pasture.

35.—*Use of Schoolroom Free of Charge.* (1) Any room in a public elementary school in respect of which a grant is made out of moneys provided by Parliament may, except while the room is being used for educational purposes, be used free of charge for the purposes of this Part of this Act by the county council, or, with the consent of any two managers, for the purpose of holding public meetings to discuss any question relating to allotments under this Act, but any damage done to the room and any expense incurred by the persons having control over the room on account of its being so used shall be paid by the county council or the persons calling the meeting.

(2) Nothing in this section shall give any right to hold a public meeting in a schoolroom—

(a) unless not less than six days before the meeting a notice of the intention to hold the meeting on the day and at the time specified in the notice, signed by the persons calling the meeting, being not less than six in number, and being persons qualified to make a representation to the council of a borough, urban district, or parish under this Part of this Act, has been given, in the case of a school provided by the local education authority to the clerk of that authority, and in any other case to one of the managers of the school; or

(b) if the use of the schoolroom on the said day and at the said time has previously to the receipt of the notice of the meeting been granted for some other purpose; but in that case the clerk or manager, or some one on his behalf, shall forthwith, after the receipt of the notice, inform in writing one of the persons signing it that the use of the school has been so granted for some other purpose, and name some other day on which the schoolroom can be used for the meeting.

(3) If the persons calling the meeting fail to obtain the use of a schoolroom under this section, they may appeal to the small holdings and allotments committee under this Act, and the committee shall forthwith decide the appeal, and make such order respecting the use of the room as seems just.

(4) Nothing in this section shall affect the powers as to the use of schoolrooms conferred by section four of the Local Government Act, 1894.

36.—*Application to London.* The powers as to allotments conferred on borough, urban district, and parish councils by this Act may in London be exercised by the London County Council, and the provisions of this Act as to allotments shall apply accordingly, except that, subject to the provisions of this Act, the expenses shall be defrayed and money borrowed under and in accordance with the provisions of the Local Government Act, 1888.

37.—*Application to County Boroughs.* Such of the provisions of this Part of this Act as require the sanction of, submission to, or order of, a county council shall not apply in the case of a county borough.

## Part III.

38.—*Purchase of Land by Agreement.* For the purpose of the purchase of land by agreement under this Act by a council, the Lands Clauses Acts shall be incorporated with this Act, except the provisions of those Acts with respect to the purchase and taking of land otherwise than by agreement, and section one hundred and seventy-eight of the Public Health Act, 1875, shall apply as if the council were referred to therein.

39.—*Procedure for Compulsory Acquisition of Land.* (1) Where a council propose to purchase land compulsorily under this Act, the council may, subject to the provisions of Part I of the First Schedule to this Act, submit to the Board an order putting in force as respects the land specified in the order the provisions of the Lands Clauses Acts with respect to the purchase and taking of land otherwise than by agreement.

(2) Where a council propose to hire land compulsorily, the council may submit to the Board an order for the compulsory hiring of the land specified in the order for a period not less than fourteen nor more than thirty-five years, and the provisions of Part I of the First Schedule to this Act shall apply to the order in like manner as it applies to an order for compulsory purchase, with the substitution of " hiring " for " purchase," and with the modifications set out in Part II of that Schedule.

(3) An order under this section shall be of no force unless and until it is confirmed by the Board, and the Board may, subject to the provisions of the First Schedule to this Act, confirm the order either without modification or subject to such modifications as they think fit, and an order when so confirmed shall become final and have effect as if enacted in this Act ; and the confirmation by the Board shall be conclusive evidence that the requirements of this Act have been complied with, and that the order has been duly made and is within the powers of this Act.

(4) An order under this section may provide for the continuance of any existing easement or the creation of any new easement over the land authorized to be acquired, and every such order shall, if so required by the owner of the land to be acquired, provide for the creation of such new easements as are reasonably necessary to secure the continued use and enjoyment by such owner and his tenants of all means of access, drainage, water supply, and other similar conveniences theretofore used or enjoyed by them over the land to be acquired : Provided that, notwithstanding anything contained in this subsection, no new easement created by or in pursuance of the order over land hired by a council shall continue beyond the determination of such hiring.

(5) In determining the amount of any disputed compensation under any such order, no additional allowance shall be made on account of the purchase or hiring being compulsory.

(6) Where land authorized to be compulsorily hired by an

order under this section is subject to a mortgage, any lease made in pursuance of the order by the mortgagor or mortgagee in possession shall have the like effect as if it were a lease authorized by section eighteen of the Conveyancing and Law of Property Act, 1881.

(7) Where the council proposing to acquire land compulsorily is a parish council, the council shall, instead of themselves making and submitting to the Board the order, represent the case to the county council, and thereupon the county council may, on behalf of the parish council, exercise the powers in relation to compulsory purchase or hiring conferred on councils by this Act, and the order shall be carried into effect by the county council, but the land shall be assured or demised to the parish council, and all expenses incurred by the county council shall be paid by the parish council :

Provided that, if the parish council are aggrieved by the refusal of the county council to proceed under this section, the parish council may petition the Board, and thereupon the Board, after such inquiry as they think fit, may make such an order as the county council might have made, and this subsection shall apply as if the order had been made by the county council.

(8) If, after the determination of the amount of the compensation (including in the case of land hired compulsorily the rent) to be paid to any person in respect of his interest in the land proposed to be compulsorily acquired, it appears to the council that the land cannot be let for small holdings or allotments, as the case may be, at such a rent as will secure the council from loss, the council may at any time within six weeks after the determination of the amount by notice in writing withdraw any notice to treat served on that person or on any other person interested in the land, and in such case any person on whom such a notice of withdrawal has been served shall be entitled to obtain from the council compensation for any loss or expenses which he may have sustained or incurred by reason or in consequence of the notice to treat and of the notice of withdrawal, and the amount of such compensation shall, in default of agreement, be determined by arbitration :

Provided that in every case in which the notice of withdrawal is given by the Commissioners acting in default of the council all compensation payable under this subsection shall be paid out of the Small Holdings Account.

40.—*Powers of Certain Limited Owners to Sell and Lease Land for Allotments.* (1) Any person having power to lease land for agricultural purposes for a limited term, whether subject to any consent or conditions or not, may, subject to the like consent and conditions (if any), lease land to a council for the purposes of small holdings or allotments for a term not exceeding thirty-five years, either with or without such right of renewal as is conferred by this Act in the case of land hired compulsorily for those purposes.

(2) The like powers of leasing may be exercised, in the case of land belonging to the Crown, by the Commissioners of Woods, with the consent of the Treasury, in the case of land forming part of the possessions of the Duchy of Lancaster, by the Chancellor and Council of the Duchy of Lancaster by deed under the seal of the Duchy in the name of His Majesty His heirs and successors, and, in the case of land forming part of the possessions of the Duchy of Cornwall, by the Duke of Cornwall or other the persons for the time being having power to dispose of land belonging to that Duchy.

(3) The like powers of leasing may be exercised in the case of glebe land or other land belonging to an ecclesiastical benefice by the incumbent thereof with the consent of the Ecclesiastical Commissioners alone upon such terms and conditions and in such manner as the Ecclesiastical Commissioners may approve.

41.—*Restrictions on the Acquisition of Land.* (1) No land shall be authorized by an order under this Act to be acquired compulsorily which at the date of the order forms part of any park, garden, or pleasure ground, or forms part of the home farm attached to and usually occupied with a mansion house, or is otherwise required for the amenity or convenience of any dwelling-house, or which is woodland not wholly surrounded by or adjacent to land acquired by a council under this Act, or which at that date is the property of any local authority or has been acquired by any corporation or company for the purposes of a railway, dock, canal, water, or other public undertaking, or is the site of an ancient monument or other object of archæological interest.

(2) A council in making, and the Board in confirming, an order for the compulsory acquisition of land shall have regard to the extent of land held or occupied in the locality by any owner or tenant and to the convenience of other property belonging to or occupied by the same owner or tenant, and shall, so far as practicable, avoid taking an undue or inconvenient quantity of land from any one owner or tenant, and for that purpose, where part only of a holding is taken, shall take into consideration the size and character of the existing agricultural buildings not proposed to be taken which were used in connection with the holding, and the quantity and nature of the land available for occupation therewith, and shall also, so far as practicable, avoid displacing any considerable number of agricultural labourers or others employed on or about the land.

(3) (Repealed by the Act of 1919.)

SMALL HOLDINGS AND ALLOTMENTS ACT, 1908

42.—*Grazing Rights, etc., to be Attached to Allotments.* (1) The powers of a council to acquire land for small holdings or allotments shall, subject to the restrictions by this Act imposed, include power to acquire land for the purpose of [attaching to] **letting to tenants of** small holdings [or] **and** allotments [provided by the council] rights of grazing and other similar rights over the land so acquired, and to acquire for that purpose stints and other alienable common rights of grazing.

(2) Any rights created or acquired by the council under this section shall be **let to tenants of** [attached to the] small holdings or allotments in such manner and subject to such regulations as the council think expedient.

44.—*Power of Council to Renew Tenancy of Land Compulsorily Hired.* (1) Where a council has hired land compulsorily for small holdings or allotments, the council may, by giving to the landlord not more than two years nor less than one year before the expiration of the tenancy notice in writing, renew the tenancy for such term, not being less than fourteen nor more than thirty-five years, as may be specified in the notice, and at such rent as, in default of agreement, may be determined by valuation by a valuer appointed by the Board, but otherwise on the same terms and conditions as the original lease, and so from time to time :

Provided that, if on any such notice being given, the landlord proves to the satisfaction of the Board that any land included in the tenancy is required for the amenity or convenience of any dwelling-house, then such land shall be excluded from the renewed tenancy.

(2) In assessing the rent to be paid under this section the valuer shall not take into account any increase in the value of the holding—
- (a) due to improvements in respect of which the council would have been entitled to compensation, if instead of renewing the tenancy the council had quitted the land on the determination of the tenancy : or
- (b) due to any use to which the land might otherwise be put during the renewed term, being a use in respect of which the landlord is entitled to resume possession of the land under this Act ;
- (c) due to the establishment by the council of other small holdings or allotments in the neighbourhood, or any depreciation in the value of the land in respect of which the landlord would have been entitled to compensation if the council had so quitted the land as aforesaid.

45.—*Interchange of Land for Small Holdings and Allotments.* A county council may sell or let to a borough, urban

F

district, or parish council for the purpose of allotments any land acquired by them for small holdings, and a borough, urban district, or parish council may sell or let to the county council for the purpose of small holdings any land acquired by them for allotments, and the provisions of the Lands Clauses Acts with respect to the sale of superfluous land shall not apply on any such sale.

46.—*Power to Resume Possession of Land Hired Compulsorily.* (1) Where land has been hired by a council compulsorily for small holdings or allotments, and the land or any part thereof at any time during the tenancy thereof by the council is shown to the satisfaction of the Board to be required by the landlord to be used for building, mining, or other industrial purposes, or for roads necessary therefor, it shall be lawful for the landlord to resume possession of the land or part thereof upon giving to the council twelve months' previous notice in writing of his intention so to do, **or such shorter notice as may be required by the order for the compulsory hiring of the land ;** and, if a part only of the land is resumed, the rent payable by the council shall as from the date of resumption be reduced by such sum as in default of agreement may be determined by valuation by a valuer appointed by the Board.

(2) Where the land has been hired compulsorily by the Commissioners acting in default of a county council, any question as to the right of the landlord to resume possession of the land or any part thereof under this section shall be determined by an arbitrator appointed by the Lord Chief Justice of England.

47.—*Compensation for Improvements.* (1) Where a council has let a small holding or allotment to any tenant, the tenant shall as against the council have the same rights with respect to compensation for the improvements mentioned in Part I of the Second Schedule to this Act as he would have had if the holding had been a holding to which section forty-two of the Agricultural Holdings Act, 1908, applied :

Provided that the tenant shall not be entitled to compensation in respect of any such improvement if executed contrary to an express prohibition in writing by the council affecting either the whole or any part of the holding or allotment ; but, if the tenant feels aggrieved by any such prohibition, he may appeal to the Board, who may confirm, vary, or annul the prohibition, and the decision of the Board shall be final.

(2) Where land has been hired by a council for small holdings or allotments, the council shall [(subject in the case of land hired by agreement to any agreement to the contrary)] **subject to any provisions to the contrary in the agreement or order for hiring** be entitled at the deter-

## SMALL HOLDINGS AND ALLOTMENTS ACT, 1908    73

mination of the tenancy on quitting the land to compensation under the Agricultural Holdings Act, 1908, for any improvement mentioned in Part I of the Second Schedule to this Act, and for any improvement mentioned in Part II of that Schedule which was necessary or proper to adapt the land for small holdings or allotments, as if the land were a holding to which section forty-two of the Agricultural Holdings Act, 1908, applied, and the improvements mentioned in Part II of the said Schedule were improvements mentioned in Part III of the First Schedule to the Agricultural Holdings Act, 1908 :

Provided that, in the case of land hired compulsorily, the amount of the compensation payable to the council for those improvements shall be such sum as fairly represents the increase (if any) in the value to the landlord and his successors in title of the holding due to those improvements.

(3) The tenant of an allotment to which Part II of this Act applies may, if he so elects, claim compensation for improvements under the Allotments and Cottage Gardens Compensation for Crops Act, 1887, instead of under the Agricultural Holdings Act, 1908, as amended by this section, notwithstanding that the allotment exceeds two acres in extent.

(4) A tenant of any small holding or allotment may, before the expiration of his tenancy, remove any fruit and other trees and bushes planted or acquired by him for which he has no claim for compensation, and may remove any toolhouse, shed, greenhouse, fowl-house or pigsty built or acquired by him for which he has no claim for compensation.

48.—*Provisions as to Glebe Lands.* In the case of glebe land or other land belonging to an ecclesiastical benefice hired by a council for the purposes of small holdings or allotments—

(1) The provisions of the Ecclesiastical Dilapidations Act, 1871, shall not during the continuance of the tenancy be applicable to the buildings upon the land :

(2) At the determination of the tenancy, on the council quitting the land, or at any time within twelve months thereafter, the incumbent of the benefice to which the land belongs may apply to the Ecclesiastical Commissioners for their consent to the removal of any buildings, which have been erected on the land for the purpose of adapting the land for small holdings or allotments, and, on proof to the satisfaction of the Commissioners that any such buildings are useless and that it is to the interest of the benefice that they should be removed, the incumbent may, with the consent of the Commissioners, and subject to such directions as they

may give, pull down any such buildings and dispose of the materials thereof, and any proceeds shall be paid to the Commissioners to be by them applied to the improvement of the benefice in such manner as the Commissioners may direct.

49.—*Co-operative Societies, etc.* (1) A county **or borough or urban district** council may promote the formation or extension of, and may, subject to the provisions of this section, assist, societies on a co-operative basis, having for their object, or one of their objects, the provision or the profitable working of small holdings or allotments, whether in relation to the purchase of requisites, the sale of produce, credit banking, or insurance, or otherwise, and may employ as their agents for the purpose any such society as is mentioned in subsection (4) of this section.

(2) The county **or borough or urban district** council, with the consent of, and subject to regulations made by, the Local Government Board, may for the purpose of assisting a society make grants or advances to the society, or guarantee advances made to the society, upon such terms and conditions as to rate of interest and repayment or otherwise, and on such security, as the council think fit.

(4) The Board with the consent of the Treasury may out of the Small Holdings Account make grants, upon such terms as the Board may determine, to any society having as its object or one of its objects the promotion of co-operation in connection with the cultivation of small holdings or allotments.

50.—*Small Holdings and Allotments Committees.* (1) Every county council shall establish a small holdings and allotments committee, consisting either wholly or partly of members of the council, but the members of the council shall be a majority, and all matters relating to the exercise and performance by the council of their powers and duties under this Act (except the power of raising a rate or borrowing money) shall stand referred to the small holdings and allotments committee, and the council before exercising any such powers shall, unless in their opinion the matter is urgent, receive and consider the report of the small holdings and allotments committee with respect to the matter in question, and the council may also delegate to the small holdings and allotments committee, with or without restrictions or conditions, as they think fit, any of their powers under this Act except the power of raising a rate or borrowing money.

(2) The small holdings and allotments committee may delegate any of their powers to sub-committees, consisting either wholly or partly of members of the committee, and in appointing any sub-committee to which is committed the powers of management of small holdings shall have regard to the advisability of including amongst the members of the

sub-committee members of the councils of the boroughs, urban districts, or parishes in which the holdings are situate, or for which they are provided, and other persons acquainted with the needs and circumstances of the area for which the sub-committee act.

(3) Where any receipts or payments of money under this Act are entrusted by the county council to the small holdings and allotments committee, or any sub-committee thereof, the accounts of those receipts and payments shall be accounts of the county council, and made up and audited accordingly.

(4) This section, so far as relates to small holdings, shall apply to the council of a county borough in like manner as it applies to a county council, but, so far as it relates to allotments and sub-committees, shall not apply to the council of a county borough, without prejudice however to the power of such a council to appoint their small holdings committee, if duly qualified, to be allotment managers in pursuance of Part II of this Act.

53.—*Expenses and Borrowing.* (1) All expenses incurred by the council of a borough, urban district, or parish under the provisions of this Act relating to allotments, including allowances to officers of the council for duties under those provisions, and any sums under those provisions repayable by a district or parish council to a county council acting in their default, shall be defrayed—

(*a*) in the case of a borough or urban district council, as part of the general expenses of their execution of the Public Health Acts ; and

(*b*) in the case of a parish council, as part of the expenses of the council.

(2) All expenses incurred by the county council in executing the said provisions in any district or parish in default of a district or parish council, or incurred by the county council in or incidentally to a local inquiry under those provisions, shall be paid in the first instance out of the county fund as expenses for general county purposes, and, unless defrayed out of moneys received by the council in respect of any land acquired under those provisions otherwise than by sale or exchange, or out of money borrowed as before in this Act mentioned, shall, when the powers and duties of the district or parish council under those provisions are transferred to the county council in pursuance of this Act, be repaid to the county council as a debt by the district or parish council.

(4) The council of a borough, urban district, or parish may borrow for the purposes of acquiring, improving, and adapting land for allotments, **and the council of a borough or urban district may borrow for the purpose of grants or advances to a co-operative society—**

(*a*) in the case of a borough or urban district council, in like manner and subject to the like conditions as for the purposes of the Public Health Acts; and

(b) in the case of a parish council, under and in accordance with the provisions of the Local Government Act, 1894, but the money so borrowed by a parish council shall not be reckoned as part of the debt of the parish for the purpose of the limitation on borrowing under section twelve of that Act.

(5) Sections two hundred and forty-two and two hundred and forty-three of the Public Health Act, 1875, relating to loans by the Public Works Loan Commissioners to a local authority, shall apply to a loan to a borough or urban district council under this section, and, with the necessary adaptations, to a loan to a parish council under the Local Government Act, 1894, or to a county council lending money to a parish council under that Act, where the purpose for which the loan is required by the parish council is the acquisition, improvement, or adaptation of land under Part II of this Act, in like manner as if those sections were herein re-enacted and in terms made applicable thereto.

54.—*Separate Accounts of Receipts and Expenditure.* (1) Separate accounts shall be kept of the receipts and expenditure of a council under this Act with respect to small holdings or allotments, and any such receipts shall, subject to the provisions of this Act, be applicable to the purposes of small holdings or allotments, but not for any other purpose except with the consent of the Local Government Board; and, for the purpose of the provisions relating to the audit of accounts, any persons appointed under this Act by a council to exercise and perform powers and duties as to the management of allotments shall be deemed to be officers of the council.

(2) The council of a borough, urban district, or parish shall within one month after the end of every financial year of the council cause an annual statement, showing their receipts and expenditure with respect to allotments for that year and their liabilities outstanding at the end of that year, to be deposited at some convenient place in the borough, district, or parish, and any ratepayer may without fee inspect and take copies of the statement.

55.—*Provisions as to Land Acquired by Commissioners.* Any land acquired by the Commissioners under this Act or any enactment repealed by this Act shall be vested in the Board, but the Board may at any time transfer the land to the council at whose expense the land was acquired, and shall so transfer the land on payment of all sums due from the council in connection therewith, and on proof to the satisfaction of the Board that the Council are willing to exercise and perform their powers and duties in relation thereto.

56.—*Provisions as to Commissioners.* Anything by this

# SMALL HOLDINGS AND ALLOTMENTS ACT, 1908

Act required or authorized to be done by or to the Commissioners may be done by or to any one such Commissioner, and any document purporting to be signed by a Commissioner shall be received in evidence without proof of the appointment or handwriting of the Commissioner.

57.—*Local Inquiries.* (1) The Board and the Small Holdings Commissioners and other officers of the Board shall have for the purpose of an inquiry in pursuance of this Act the same powers as the Local Government Board and their inspectors respectively have for the purpose of an inquiry under the Public Health Acts.

(2) Notices of the inquiries shall be given and published in accordance with such general or special directions as the Board may give.

(3) A local inquiry by a county council for the purposes of the provisions of this Act relating to allotments shall be held by such one or more members of the small holdings and allotments committee of the council or by such officer of the council or other person as that committee may appoint to hold the inquiry.

58.—*Arbitrations and Valuations.* (1) All questions which under this Act are referred to arbitration shall, unless otherwise expressly provided by this Act, be determined by a single arbitrator in accordance with the Agricultural Holdings [(England)] Act, 1908.

(2) Where an order has been made and confirmed authorizing the compulsory acquisition of land by the Commissioners acting in default of a county council, the arbitrator or valuer, as the case may be, shall be appointed by the Lord Chief Justice of England instead of by the Board.

(3) The remuneration of an arbitrator or valuer appointed under this Act shall be fixed by the Board.

59.—*Annual Report to Parliament.* The Board shall make an annual report to Parliament of their proceedings, and of the proceedings of the Commissioners, under this Act, and also of the proceedings of the several county, borough, district, and parish councils under this Act, and for that purpose every such council shall, before such date in every year as the Board may fix, send to the Board a report of their proceedings under this Act during the preceding year.

60.—*Saving for Existing Tenancies.* Nothing in this Act shall affect the rights and obligations under any tenancy created under any enactment repealed by this Act.

61.—*Interpretation.* (1) For the purposes of this Act—
The expression " allotment " includes a field garden :
The expressions " agriculture " and " cultivation " shall include horticulture and the use of land for any purpose of husbandry, inclusive of the keeping or breeding of live stock, poultry, or bees, and the growth of fruit, vegetables, and the like :

The expression "county" shall mean the area under the authority of a county council:

The expression "prescribed" means prescribed by regulations made by the Board:

The expression "landlord," in relation to any land compulsorily hired by a council, means the person for the time being entitled to receive the rent of the land from the council.

(2) In this Act and in the enactments incorporated with this Act the expression "land" shall include any right or easement in or over land.

(3) For the purposes of this Act, any expenses incurred by a council in the enfranchisement of any land acquired by them for small holdings or allotments, or in the purchase or redemption of land tax, or any quit rent, chief rent, tithe, or other rentcharge, or other perpetual annual sum issuing out of land so acquired, shall be deemed to have been incurred in the purchase of the land.

(4) In this Act references to a parish council shall, in the case of a rural parish not having a parish council, include references to the parish meeting.

(5) Any notice required by this Act to be served or given may be sent by registered post.

62.—*Repeal.* The enactments mentioned in the Third Schedule to this Act are hereby repealed to the extent specified in the third column of that Schedule.

Provided that—

(a) Nothing in this Act shall affect any order, scheme, draft scheme, rules, regulations, report, petition, notice, or other document made, prepared, submitted, served, or given under any enactment so repealed, but every such document shall have effect as if made, prepared, submitted, served, or given under this Act ; and

(b) References in any conveyance, lease, or other document to any enactment so repealed shall have effect as if they had been references to the corresponding provisions of this Act ; and

(c) If any question arises as to whether any power of the Local Government Board under the enactments relating to allotments hereby repealed was thereby transferred to the Board of Agriculture and Fisheries, the question shall be determined by the Local Government Board, whose decision shall be final.

63.—*Short Title, Commencement, and Extent.* (1) This Act may be cited as the Small Holdings and Allotments Act, 1908.

(2) This Act shall come into operation on the first day of January one thousand nine hundred and nine.

(3) This Act shall not extend to Scotland or Ireland.

## SCHEDULES.

### FIRST SCHEDULE.

#### PART I.

PROVISIONS AS TO THE COMPULSORY ACQUISITION OF LAND BY A COUNCIL.

(1) The order shall be in the prescribed form, and shall contain such provisions as the Board may prescribe for the purpose of carrying the order into effect, and of protecting the council and the persons interested in the land, and shall incorporate, subject to the necessary adaptations, the Lands Clauses Acts and sections seventy-seven to eighty-five of the Railways Clauses Consolidation Act, 1845, but subject to this modification, that any question of disputed compensation shall be determined by a single arbitrator appointed by the Board, who shall be deemed to be an arbitrator within the meaning of the Lands Clauses Acts, and the provisions of those Acts with respect to arbitration shall, subject to the provisions of this schedule, apply accordingly.

(2) The order shall be published by the council in the prescribed manner, and such notice shall be given both in the locality in which the land is proposed to be acquired and to the owners, lessees, and occupiers of that land, as may be prescribed.

(3) If within the prescribed period no objection to the order has been presented to the Board by a person interested in the land, or if every such objection has been withdrawn, the Board shall, without further inquiry confirm the order, but, if such an objection has been presented and has not been withdrawn, the Board shall forthwith cause a public inquiry to be held in the locality in which the land is proposed to be acquired, and the council and all persons interested in the land and such other persons as the person holding the inquiry in his discretion thinks fit to allow shall be permitted to appear and be heard at the inquiry.

(4) Before confirming the order the Board shall consider the report of the person who held the inquiry, and all objections made thereat.

(5) The arbitrator shall, so far as practicable, in assessing compensation act on his own knowledge and experience, but, subject as aforesaid, at any inquiry or arbitration held under this schedule the person holding the inquiry or arbitration shall hear, by themselves or their agents, any authorities or parties authorized by or under this Act to appear, and shall

hear witnesses, but shall not, except in such cases as the Board otherwise direct, hear counsel or expert witnesses.

(6) The Board may, with the concurrence of the Lord Chancellor, make rules fixing a scale of costs to be applicable on an arbitration under this schedule, and an arbitrator under this schedule may, notwithstanding anything in the Lands Clauses Acts, determine the amount of costs, and shall have power to disallow as costs in the arbitration the costs of any witness whom he considers to have been called unnecessarily, and any other costs which he considers to have been caused or incurred unnecessarily.

(7) In construing, for the purposes of this schedule or any order made thereunder, any enactment incorporated with the order, this Act together with the order shall be deemed to be the special Act and the council shall be deemed to be the promoters of the undertaking.

(8) Where the land is glebe land or other land belonging to an ecclesiastical benefice the order shall provide that sums agreed upon or awarded for the purchase of the land, or to be paid by way of compensation for the damage to be sustained by the owner by reason of severance or other injury affecting the land, shall not be paid as directed by the Lands Clauses Acts, but shall be paid to the Ecclesiastical Commissioners to be applied by them as money paid to them upon a sale under the provisions of the Ecclesiastical Leasing Acts of land belonging to a benefice.

## Part II.

### Provisions as to the Compulsory Hiring of Land by a Council.

(1) The Board shall make regulations for the purpose of carrying the order into effect and of protecting the council and the persons interested in the land, and the order shall incorporate such regulations, together with such provisions of the Lands Clauses Acts and of sections seventy-seven to eighty-five of the Railways Clauses Consolidation Act, 1845, as may, subject to the prescribed adaptations, appear to the Board necessary or expedient for that purpose.

(2) The order authorizing the land to be hired compulsorily shall determine the terms and conditions of the hiring other than the rent, and in particular—

(a) shall provide for the insertion in the lease of covenants by the council to cultivate the land in a proper manner and to pay to the landlord at the determination of the tenancy on the council quitting the land compensation for any depreciation of the land by reason of any failure by the council, or any person deriving title under them, to observe such covenants, or by reason of any user of the land by the council or such person as aforesaid and (unless otherwise agreed) to keep the buildings and premises demised in repair ; and

(b) shall not authorize the breaking up of pasture unless the Board are satisfied that it can be so broken up without depreciating the value of the land, or that the circumstances are such that small holdings **or allotments as the case may be** cannot otherwise be successfully cultivated ; and

(c) shall not, except with the consent of the landlord, confer on the council any right to fell or cut timber or trees or any right to take, sell, or carry away any minerals, gravel, sand, or clay, except so far as may be necessary or convenient for the purpose of erecting buildings on the land or otherwise adapting the land for small holdings or allotments, and except upon payment of compensation for minerals, gravel, sand, or clay so used.

(3) The determination of—

(a) the amount of the rent to be paid by the council for the land compulsorily hired ;

(b) the amount of any other compensation to be paid by the council to any person entitled thereto in respect of the land or any interest therein, or in respect of improvements executed on the land or otherwise ; and

(c) where part only of a holding held for an unexpired term is hired, the rent to be paid for the residue of the holding during the remainder of that term ;

shall in default of agreement be by valuation by a single valuer appointed by the Board : Provided that if the land hired is in the occupation of a tenant, he may by notice in writing served on the council before the determination of his tenancy, require that any claim by him against the council which, under the Agricultural Holdings Act, 1908, might be referred to arbitration under that Act, shall be so referred, and in such case those claims shall be determined by arbitration **under that Act** and not by valuation under this Act.

(4) The valuer, in fixing the rent to be paid for the land compulsorily hired, shall take into consideration the rent (if any) at which the land has been let and the annual value at which the land is assessed for purposes of income tax or rating, the loss (if any) caused to the owner by severance, the terms and conditions of the hiring (including any reservation of sporting or fishing rights), and all the other circumstances

connected with the land, but shall not make any allowance in respect of any use to which the land compulsorily hired might otherwise be put by the owner during the term of hiring, being a use in respect of which the owner is entitled to resume possession of the land under this Act.

(5) Any compensation awarded to a tenant in respect of any depreciation of the value to him of the residue of his holding caused by the withdrawal from the holding of the land compulsorily hired shall, as far as possible, be provided for by taking such compensation into account in fixing the rent to be paid for the residue of the holding during the remainder of the term for which it is held by the tenant.

(6) Any person interested in any valuation shall give the valuer all such assistance, information, and explanations as he may require, and shall produce to the valuer, or give him access to, all such books, accounts, vouchers, and other documents relating to the land to be compulsorily hired as he may reasonably require for the purposes of valuation, and such expenses **as the council shall consider or** as the valuer certifies to have been properly incurred by any person in furnishing such assistance, information, and explanations, or otherwise, in relation to the valuation, shall be paid by the council.

(7) On the determination of any tenancy created by compulsory hiring any questions as to the amount due by the council for depreciation shall in default of agreement be determined by arbitration.

## SECOND SCHEDULE.

Improvements referred to in Section Forty-seven.

### Part I.

(1) Planting of standard or other fruit trees permanently set out;
(2) Planting of fruit bushes permanently set out;
(3) Planting of strawberry plants;
(4) Planting of asparagus, rhubarb, and other vegetable crops which continue productive for two or more years.

### Part II.

(1) Erection, alteration, or enlargement of buildings;
(2) Formation of silos;
(3) Laying down of permanent pasture;
(4) Making and planting of osier beds;
(5) Making of water meadows or works of irrigation;

## SMALL HOLDINGS AND ALLOTMENTS ACT, 1908

(6) Making of gardens;
(7) Making or improving roads or bridges;
(8) Making or improving of watercourses, ponds, wells, or reservoirs, or of works for the application of water power or for supply of water for agricultural or domestic purposes:
(9) Making or removal of permanent fences;
(10) Planting of hops;
(11) Planting of orchards or fruit bushes;
(12) Protecting young fruit-trees;
(13) Reclaiming of waste land;
(14) Warping or weiring of land;
(15) Embankments and sluices against floods;
(16) The erection of wirework in hop gardens;
(17) Drainage.

### THIRD SCHEDULE.

ENACTMENTS REPEALED (section 62.)

| Short Title. | Extent of Repeal. |
| --- | --- |
| The Allotments Act, 1887. | The whole Act, except as respects subsections (4) to (8) of section three so far as they are applied by any other enactment. |
| The Allotments Act, 1890. | The whole Act. |
| The Small Holdings Act, 1892. | The whole Act, except so far as it relates to Scotland. |
| The Local Government Act, 1894. | In section six, subsections (3) and (4). |
| The Land Transfer Act, 1897. | Section nineteen. |
| The Small Holdings and Allotments Act, 1907. | The whole Act. |

(II)

## LAND SETTLEMENT (FACILITIES) ACT, 1919.

(9 & 10 GEO. 5, CH. 59.)

**(19th August, 1919.)**

(So far as it relates to allotments.)

Be it enacted, etc.

## APPENDIX

### Part I.

#### Provisions as to the Acquisition of Land.

1.—*Temporary Suspension of Requirements as to Confirmation of Orders for the Acquisition of Land.* (1) Any order for the compulsory acquisition of land which is duly made after the date of the passing of this Act and before the expiration of three years from that date by a council under the Small Holdings and Allotments Act, 1908 (hereinafter referred to as the principal Act), need not, except as otherwise expressly provided by this Act, be submitted to or confirmed by the Board of Agriculture and Fisheries, but shall have effect as if it had been so confirmed:

Provided that a grant or inclosure of common purporting to be made under any such order shall not be valid unless it is made with the consent of the Board, given under and in accordance with the provisions of section twenty-two of the Commons Act, 1899.

(2) Notice of the making of an order to which this section applies shall be given in the prescribed form and manner by the council as soon as practicable to each owner, lessee, and occupier of the land authorized to be acquired, and a copy of the order and of any plan annexed or referred to in the order shall be furnished by the council to any person interested in the land, on application by such person.

2.—*Power of Entry on Land.* (1) Where an order for the compulsory purchase of land has been made, and where necessary confirmed, under the principal Act, whether such order was made before or after the passing of this Act, the council entitled to purchase the land under the order may, at any time after a notice to treat has been served, and on giving not less than fourteen days' notice to each owner, lessee and occupier of the land, enter on and take possession of the land or such part thereof as is specified in the notice without previous consent or compliance with sections eighty-four to ninety of the Lands Clauses (Consolidation) Act, 1845, but subject to the payment of the like compensation for the land of which possession is taken and interest thereon as would have been payable if the provisions of those sections had been complied with:

Provided that, where a council have so entered on land, the council shall not be entitled to exercise the powers conferred by subsection (8) of section thirty-nine of the principal Act.

(2) Where a council have agreed, for the purposes of the principal Act, to purchase land subject to the interest of the person in possession thereof, and that interest is not greater than that of a tenant for a year, or from year to year, then at any time after such agreement has been made the council may,

after giving not less than fourteen days' notice to the person so in possession, enter on and take possession of the land or of such part thereof as is specified in the notice without previous consent, but subject to the payment to the person so in possession of the like compensation for the land of which possession is taken, with such interest thereon as aforesaid, as if the council had been authorized to purchase the land compulsorily and such person had, in pursuance of such power, been required to quit possession before the expiration of his term or interest in the land, but without the necessity of compliance with sections eighty-four to ninety of the Lands Clauses (Consolidation) Act, 1845.

(3) Where a notice of entry under this section relates to land on which there is a dwelling-house and the length of notice is less than three calendar months, the occupier of the dwelling-house may, by notice served on the council within ten days after the service on him of the notice of entry, appeal against such notice, and in any such case the appeal shall be determined by an arbitrator under and in accordance with the provisions of the Second Schedule of the Agricultural Holdings Act, 1908 (except that the arbitrator shall, in default of agreement, be appointed by the President of the Surveyors' Institution), and the council shall not be entitled to enter on the land under this section except on such date and on such conditions as the arbitrator may award.

(4) This section shall with such necessary adaptations as may be prescribed apply in the case of an order authorizing the compulsory hiring of land, or of an agreement to hire land.

3.—*Power of Board of Agriculture and Fisheries to Provide Land for Settlement.*
[*Note.*—The powers of the Board to provide land for leasing to a parish council for the provision of allotments under this section have now lapsed.]

8.—*Sales of Glebe.* For the purpose of a sale of land under the Ecclesiastical Leasing Acts to a council or to the Board of Agriculture and Fisheries for the purposes of the principal Act or the Small Holdings Colonies Acts, 1916 and 1918, the consent of the patron to the sale shall not be necessary.

## Part II.

### Amendment of the Small Holdings and Allotments Act, 1908.

12.—(3) The provisions of the Lands Clauses (Consolidation) Act, 1845, with respect to the sale of superfluous land, shall not apply to land acquired by a council under the principal Act.

86    APPENDIX

16.—*Amendment of Section 41 of Principal Act.* (1) An order under the principal Act may, notwithstanding anything in section forty-one thereof, authorize the compulsory acquisition—

(a) of any land which at the date of the order forms part of any park or of any home farm attached to and usually occupied with a mansion house, if the land is not required for the amenity or convenience of the mansion house ; or

(b) of a holding of fifty acres or less in extent or any part of such a holding.

(2) Where it is proposed to acquire any land forming part of a park or any such home farm, or, except where required for purposes of allotments, a holding of fifty acres or less in extent or of an annual value not exceeding fifty pounds for the purposes of income tax, or any part of such a holding, the order authorizing the acquisition of the land shall not be valid unless confirmed or made by the Board of Agriculture and Fisheries.

(3) A holding to which the preceding subsection applies shall not in whole or in part be compulsorily acquired under the principal Act by the Board or a council where it is shown to the satisfaction of the Board or the council, as the case may be, that the holding is the principal means of livelihood of the occupier thereof, except where the occupier is a tenant and consents to the acquisition.

17.—*Power of County Council to Acquire Land for Letting to Parish Council for Allotments.* A county council may acquire land for the purpose of leasing it to the council of a parish within the county for.the provision of allotments, and the provisions of the principal Act relating to the acquisition, and to proceedings in relation to the acquisition, of land for the purpose of providing small holdings shall apply to such acquisition as if the land were to be acquired for the provision of small holdings.

19.—*Power of Entry to Inspect Land.* A council, with a view to ascertaining whether any land is suitable for any purpose for which the council has power to acquire land under the principal Act, may by writing in that behalf authorize any person (upon production, if so required, of his authority) to enter and inspect the land specified in the authority, and anyone who obstructs or impedes any person acting under and in accordance with any such authority shall be liable on summary conviction to a fine not exceeding twenty pounds.

21.—(1) The council of any borough, urban district or parish may purchase any fruit-trees, seeds, plants, fertilizers or implements required for the purposes of allotments cultivated as gardens, whether provided by the council or otherwise, and sell any article so purchased to the cultivators, or, in the case of implements, allow their use, at a price or charge sufficient to cover the cost of purchase.

(2) The powers conferred by the preceding subsection shall be exercisable by a council only where in the opinion of the council the facilities for the purchase or hire of the articles therein referred to from a society on a co-operative basis are inadequate.

(3) Rules made by a council under section twenty-eight of the principal Act, shall, unless otherwise expressly provided, apply to an allotment, though held under a tenancy made before the rules come into operation.

(4) Any person who by any act done without lawful authority or by negligence causes damage to any crops growing on an allotment cultivated as a garden, shall be liable on summary conviction to a penalty not exceeding five pounds, but this provision shall not apply unless notice of the provision is conspicuously displayed on or near the allotment.

(5) Stamp duty shall not be payable on any lease or agreement for the letting of any allotment or garden, whether provided under the principal Act or otherwise, or on any duplicate or counterpart of any such lease or agreement where the rent does not exceed ten shillings per annum and no premium is paid.

22.—*Power of Appropriation of Land.* (1) A council of a borough, urban district, or parish may, in a case where no power of appropriation is otherwise provided, with the consent of the Board of Agriculture and Fisheries and the Local Government Board, and subject to such conditions as to the repayment of any loan obtained for the purpose of the acquisition of land or otherwise as the last-mentioned Board may impose—

(a) appropriate for the purpose of allotments any land held by the council for other purposes of the council; or

(b) appropriate for other purposes of the council land acquired by the council for allotments.

(2) This section shall apply, in the county of London, to the council of the county and to any metropolitan borough council.

23.—*Agreements as to Compensation where Land is Let for Provision of Allotments.* Where land is let for the provision of allotments either to a council under the principal Act or to an association formed for the purpose of creating or promoting the creation of allotments, the right of the council or association to claim compensation from the landlord on the determination of the tenancy shall be subject to the terms of the contract of tenancy, notwithstanding the provision of any Act to the contrary:

Provided that this section shall not prejudice or affect any right on the part of a person holding under a tenancy granted by the council or association to claim compensation from the council or association on the determination of his tenancy.

24.—*Power of Metropolitan Boroughs as to Allotments.* The powers as to allotments conferred on borough councils by the principal Act may be exercised by a metropolitan borough council, and the expenses so incurred by a council shall be defrayed, and money for such purpose may be borrowed, under and in accordance with the provisions of the Public Health (London) Act, 1891, as if such expenses were incurred by the council under that Act.

25.—*Minor Amendments of Principal Act.* (1) The provisions of the principal Act specified in the first column of the Second Schedule to this Act shall be amended in the manner specified in the second column of that schedule.

(2) Subsection (2) of section twenty-seven of the principal Act is hereby repealed.

## Part IV.

### General.

28.—*Provisions as to Commons and Open Spaces.* (1) Any land which is, or forms part of, a metropolitan common within the meaning of the Metropolitan Commons Act, 1866, or which is subject to regulation under an order or scheme made in pursuance of the Inclosure Acts, 1845 to 1899, or under any local Act or otherwise, or which is or forms part of any town or village green, or of any area dedicated or appropriated as a public park, garden, or pleasure ground, or for use for the purposes of public recreation, shall not be appropriated under this Act by a council for small holdings or allotments, and shall not be acquired by a council or by the Board of Agriculture and Fisheries under the principal Act except under the authority of an order for compulsory purchase made under the principal Act, which so far as it relates to such land shall be provisional only, and shall not have effect unless it is confirmed by Parliament.

(2) The Board of Agriculture and Fisheries, in giving or withholding their consent under this Act to the appropriation and in confirming an order for compulsory acquisition by a council for the purpose of small holdings or allotments of any land which forms part of any common, and in the exercise by the Board of their powers of acquiring land under this Act, shall have regard to the same considerations and shall hold the same inquiries as are directed by the Commons Act, 1876, to be taken into consideration and held by the Board before forming an opinion whether an application under the Inclosure Acts shall be acceded to or not. Any consent by the Board

of Agriculture and Fisheries for the appropriation of land forming part of any common for the purpose of small holdings or allotments shall be laid before Parliament while Parliament is sitting, and, if within twenty-one days in either House of Parliament a motion is carried dissenting from such appropriation, the order of the Board shall be cancelled.

(3) Where an order for compulsory purchase to which this section applies or a consent by the Board to the appropriation of land provides for giving other land in exchange for the common or open space to be purchased or appropriated, the order for compulsory purchase or an order made by the Board in relation to the consent for appropriation may vest the land given in exchange in the persons in whom the common or open space purchased or appropriated was vested subject to the same rights, trusts, and incidents as attached to the common or open space and discharges the land purchased or appropriated from all rights, trusts, and incidents to which it was previously subject.

(4) Nothing in the principal Act shall be deemed to authorize the acquisition of any land which forms part of the trust property to which the National Trust Act, 1907, applies.

29.—*Amendment of Settled Land Acts*, 1882 *to* 1890. The powers conferred upon a tenant for life by the Settled Land Acts, 1882 to 1890, shall include the following further power :—

A power at any time, or times, to make a grant or grants of any part or parts of the settled land in fee simple or absolutely, or a lease or leases for any term of years without any consideration, or at a nominal price, annuity or rent, or at less than the best price, annuity or rent that can reasonably be obtained for the purpose of the Small Holdings and Allotments Acts, 1908 to 1919, and any such grant as aforesaid shall be deemed to be a sale within the meaning of the said Settled Land Acts : Provided that, except under an order of the court, no more than two acres in the case of land situate in an urban district or ten acres in the case of land situate in a rural district in any one parish shall be granted or leased under this power for the purpose of the said Small Holdings and Allotments Acts or under the similar power conferred by the Housing, Town Planning, etc., Act, 1919, for the purpose of the erection of dwellings for the working classes or the provision of gardens to be held in connection therewith or for all of such purposes together without payment of the full-price annuity or rent for any land granted or leased in excess of such quantity.

30.—*Provisions as to Land Taken under the Defence of the Realm Regulations.* (1) For removing doubts it is hereby

90  APPENDIX

declared that section one of the Defence of the Realm (Acquisition of Land) Act, 1916, applies to land of which possession has been taken by the Board of Agriculture and Fisheries under the powers conferred by Regulations 2L and 2M of the Defence of the Realm Regulations, and that the Board are entitled whilst in possession by themselves or by any person deriving title under them of the land, after the termination of the present war, to exercise in relation thereto any of the powers conferred by those regulations for such term and subject to such conditions as are mentioned in the said Act.

(2) Where at the termination of the present war a local authority is exercising powers under the said Regulation 2L in respect of land of which the local authority is owner or occupier, the local authority may continue to exercise those powers in relation to that land until the expiration of two years from the termination of the present war, and the provisions of subsection (6) of the said regulation shall apply accordingly.

32.—*Construction.* (1) This Act, so far as it amends the principal Act, shall be construed as one with that Act, and references in this Act to the principal Act, or to any provision of the principal Act, shall, where the context permits, be construed as references to the principal Act, or the provisions of the principal Act as amended by this Act.

33.—*Repeal.* The enactments mentioned in the Third Schedule to this Act are hereby repealed to the extent specified in the third column of that schedule.

34.—*Short Title.* This Act may be cited as the Land Settlement (Facilities) Act, 1919, and the Small Holdings and Allotments Acts, 1908 and 1910, and so much of this Act as amends those Acts may be cited together as the Small Holdings and Allotments Acts, 1908 to 1919.

## SCHEDULES.

### SECOND SCHEDULE.

MINOR AMENDMENTS OF PRINCIPAL ACT (see section 25).

| Provision of the Principal Act to be amended. | Amendment. |
| --- | --- |
| Section 9 . . . | In paragraph (*b*) of subsection (2) after the word " let " there shall be inserted the words " or sell." |
| Section 23 . . | In subsection (1) the words " for the labouring population " and " belonging to the labouring population " and |

# LAND SETTLEMENT (FACILITIES) ACT, 1919

| Provision of the Principal Act to be amended. | Amendment. |
|---|---|
| Section 24 | the words from "and that such allotments cannot" to "applicants for the same" shall be omitted. Subsection (3) shall be omitted. In subsection (1) after the word "allotments" there shall be added the words "by any person or by an association to which allotments may be let under this Act" and the words "(other than boroughs)" shall be omitted. In subsection (4) the words "other than a borough" shall be omitted. |
| Section 27 | In subsection (1) after the words "quarter's rent" there shall be added the words "(except where the yearly rent is twenty shillings or less)." At the end of subsection (4) there shall be inserted the words "except with the consent of the council." In subsection (6) after the words "system or" there shall be inserted the words "of letting or selling." |
| Section 34 | In subsection (1) the word "labouring" shall be omitted. |
| Section 42 | In subsection (1) for the words "attaching to small holdings or allotments provided by the council" there shall be substituted the words "letting to tenants of small holdings and allotments," and in subsection (2) for the words "attached to the" there shall be substituted the words "let to tenants of." |
| Section 46 | In subsection (1) after the word "do" there shall be inserted the words "or such shorter notice as may be required by the order for the compulsory hiring of the land." |
| Section 47 | In subsection (2) for the words "subject in the case of land hired by agreement to any agreement to the contrary" there shall be substituted the words "subject to any provision to the contrary in the agreement or order for hiring." |

## APPENDIX

| Provision of the Principal Act to be amended. | Amendment. |
|---|---|
| Section 49 . . | In subsection (1) and subsection (2) after the word " county " in both places where it occurs there shall be inserted the words " or borough or urban district." |
| Section 53 . . | In subsection (4) after the words " adapting land for allotments " there shall be inserted the words " and the council of a borough or urban district may borrow for the purpose of grants or advances to a co-operative society." |
| Section 58 . . | In subsection (1) the word " (England) " shall be omitted. |
| Schedule I, Part II. | In paragraph (2) (b) after the word " holdings " there shall be added the words " or allotments as the case may be." In paragraph (6) after the word " expenses " there shall be added the words " as the council shall consider or." |

## THIRD SCHEDULE.

### ENACTMENTS REPEALED (section 33).

| Short Title. | Extent of Repeal. |
|---|---|
| The Small Holdings and Allotments Act, 1908. | In section twenty-three the words " for the labouring population " and " belonging to the labouring population " and the words from " and that such allotments cannot " to " applicants for the same " and subsection (3) ; in section twenty-four the words " other than boroughs " and " other than a a borough " ; subsection (2) of section twenty-seven ; section thirty-one ; subsection (3) of section thirty-two ; in section thirty-four the word " labouring " ; subsection (3) of section forty-one ; and in section fifty-eight the word " (England)." |

# (III)
# ALLOTMENTS ACT, 1922.
(12 & 13 GEO. 5, CH. 51.)
(4th August, 1922.)

ARRANGEMENT OF SECTIONS.

Section.
1. Determination of tenancies of allotment gardens.
2. Compensation on quitting allotment gardens.
3. Provision as to cottage holdings and certain allotments.
4. Further provision as to allotment gardens and allotments.
5. Rights of tenant who has paid compensation to outgoing tenant.
6. Assessment and recovery of compensation.
7. Application to Crown lands.
8. Amendment of statutory provisions as to compulsory acquisition of land for allotments.
9. Purchase of land for fee-farm rents.
10. Powers of entry on unoccupied land.
11. Determination of questions arising on resumption of land.
12. Time limit for serving notice to treat for compulsory acquisition of land.
13. Restriction of obligations of urban authorities to provide allotments.
14. Allotment committees of urban authorities.
15. Power for county councils to let land for allotments.
16. Limitation on expenditure on allotments and rents to be charged.
17. Rating of allotments.
18. Financial provisions.
19. Penalty for damage to an allotment garden.
20. Action in default of certain local authorities.
21. Provision as to parts of New Forest now used for allotment gardens.
22. Interpretation.
23. Short title, and repeal.

Be it enacted, etc.

**1.**—(1) Where land is let on a tenancy for use by the tenant as an allotment garden or is let to any local authority or association for the purpose of being sub-let for such use the tenancy of the land or any part shall not (except as hereinafter provided) be terminable by the landlord by notice to quit or re-entry, notwithstanding any agreement to the contrary, except by—

(a) a six months' or longer notice to quit expiring on or before the sixth day of April or on or after the twenty-ninth day of September in any year; or

(b) re-entry, after three months' previous notice in writing to the tenant, under a power of re-entry contained in or affecting the contract of tenancy on account of the land being required for building, mining, or any other industrial purpose or for roads or sewers necessary in connection with any of those purposes ; or

(c) re-entry under a power in that behalf contained in or affecting the contract of tenancy in the case of land let by a corporation or company being the owners or lessees of a railway, dock, canal, water, or other public undertaking on account of the land being required by the corporation, or company, for any purpose (not being the use of the land for agriculture) for which it was acquired or held by the corporation, or company, or has been appropriated under any statutory provision, but so that, except in a case of emergency, three months' notice in writing of the intended re-entry shall be given to the tenant ; or

(d) re-entry under a power in that behalf contained in or affecting the contract of tenancy, in the case of land let by a local authority (being land which was acquired by the local authority before the passing of this Act under the Housing Acts, 1890 to 1921) on account of the land being required by the local authority for the purposes of those Acts, and, in the case of other land let by a local authority, after three months' previous notice in writing to the tenant on account of the land being required by the local authority for a purpose (not being the use of land for agriculture) for which it was acquired by the local authority, or has been appropriated under any statutory provision ; or

(e) re-entry for non-payment of rent or breach of any term or condition of the tenancy or on account of the tenant becoming bankrupt or compounding with his creditors, or where the tenant is an association, on account of its liquidation.

(2) This section shall apply to a tenancy current at the date of the passing of this Act, but not so as to affect the operation of any notice to quit given, or proceedings for recovery of possession commenced, before that date.

(3) Where under any contract of tenancy to which this section applies, made before the passing of this Act, the tenancy is either by express provision or by implication made terminable by the landlord by notice to quit expiring on a date between the sixth day of April and the twenty-ninth day of September, the tenancy shall be terminable by him on the twenty-ninth day of September, and any such notice to quit given in accordance with the contract shall have the effect of a notice to·quit on that day.

(4) This section shall not apply to land held by or on behalf of the Admiralty, War Department, or Air Council, and so let as aforesaid when possession of the land is required for naval, military, or air force purposes.

**2.**—(1) Where under any contract of tenancy land is, before or after the passing of this Act, let for use by the tenant as an allotment garden, the tenant shall, subject to the provisions of this section and notwithstanding any agreement to the contrary, be entitled at the termination of the tenancy, on quitting the land, to obtain from the landlord compensation as provided by this section.

(2) Subject to the provisions of this section, compensation shall be recoverable under this section only if the tenancy is terminated by the landlord and is so terminated either—

(a) between the sixth day of April and the twenty-ninth day of September; or
(b) by re-entry at any time under paragraph (b) or paragraph (c) or paragraph (d) of subsection (1) of the last preceding section.

(3) The compensation recoverable from the landlord under this section shall be for crops growing upon the land in the ordinary course of the cultivation of the land as an allotment garden or allotment gardens, and for manure applied to the land.

(4) A tenant whose tenancy is terminated by the termination of the tenancy of his landlord shall be entitled to recover from his landlord such compensation (if any) as would have been recoverable if his tenancy had been terminated by notice to quit given by his landlord.

(5) Any sum due to the landlord from the tenant in respect of rent or of any breach of the contract of tenancy under which the land is held, or wilful or negligent damage committed or permitted by the tenant, shall be taken into account in reduction of the compensation.

(6) This section shall also apply to any contract of tenancy made after the passing of this Act by which land is let to any local authority or association for the purpose of being sublet for use by the tenants as allotment gardens and, notwithstanding that the crops have been grown and the manure applied by the tenants of the local authority or association. Section twenty-three of the Land Settlement (Facilities) Act, 1919, shall not apply to land let after the passing of this Act to any local authority or association for the purpose of being sub-let for use by the tenants as allotment gardens.

(7) This section shall apply to the termination of the tenancy of the whole or any part of the land the subject of a contract of tenancy.

(8) Except as provided by this section or by the contract of tenancy, the tenant of land under a contract of tenancy to

which this section applies shall not be entitled to recover compensation from the landlord at the termination of the tenancy.

(9) If the tenancy of the tenant is terminated on the twenty-ninth day of September or the eleventh day of October, or at any date between those days, either by notice to quit given by the landlord or by the termination of the tenancy of the landlord, the tenant whose tenancy is so terminated shall be entitled at any time within twenty-one days after the termination of the tenancy to remove any crops growing on the land.

(10) This section shall not apply to any tenancy which is terminated by the effluxion of time before the date of the passing of this Act, or, where a notice to quit has been given, re-entry has been made or proceedings for recovery of possession have been commenced before that date.

**3.**—(1) The foregoing provisions of this Act as to determination of tenancies of allotment gardens and compensation to a tenant on quitting the same shall not apply to any parcel of land attached to a cottage.

(2) In the case of any allotment within the meaning of this section (not being an allotment garden), the tenant shall, on the termination of his tenancy by effluxion of time, or from any other cause, be entitled, notwithstanding any agreement to the contrary, to obtain from the landlord compensation for the following matters:—

(a) For crops, including fruit, growing upon the land in the ordinary course of cultivation and for labour expended upon and manure applied to the land; and

(b) For fruit-trees or bushes provided and planted by the tenant with the previous consent in writing of the landlord, and for drains, outbuildings, pigsties, fowl-houses, or other structural improvements made or erected by and at the expense of the tenant on the land with such consent.

(3) Any sum due to the landlord from the tenant in respect of rent or of any breach of the contract of tenancy under which the land is held, or wilful or negligent damage committed or permitted by the tenant, shall be taken into account in reduction of the compensation.

(4) The amount of the compensation shall, in default of agreement, be determined and recovered in the same manner as compensation is, under this Act, to be determined and recovered in the case of an allotment garden.

(5) The Agricultural Holdings Acts, 1908 to 1921, shall, in the case of an allotment within the meaning of this section to which those Acts apply, have effect as if the provisions of this section as to the determination and recovery of compensation were substituted for the provisions of those Acts

as to the determination and recovery of compensation, and a claim for compensation for any matter or thing for which a claim for compensation can be made under this section, may be made either under those Acts or under this section, but not under both.

(6) The compensation in respect of an improvement made or begun on an allotment (not being an allotment garden) before the passing of this Act shall be such (if any) as could have been claimed if this Act had not been passed.

(7) In this section the expression " allotment " means any parcel of land, whether attached to a cottage or not, of not more than two acres in extent, held by a tenant under a landlord and cultivated as a farm or a garden, or partly as a garden and partly as a farm.

**4.**—(1) A tenant of land held under a contract of tenancy to which any of the foregoing provisions of this Act apply may, before the termination of the tenancy, remove any fruit-trees or bushes provided and planted by the tenant and any erection, fencing or other improvement erected or made by and at the expense of the tenant, making good any injury caused by such removal.

(2) A tenant of land held under a contract of tenancy to which any of the foregoing provisions of this Act apply and which is made with a mortgagor but is not binding on the mortgagee, shall, on being deprived of possession by the mortgagee, be entitled to recover compensation from him as if he were the landlord and had then terminated the tenancy, but subject to the deduction from such compensation of any rent or other sum due from the tenant in respect of the land.

**5.** Where a tenant of an allotment has paid compensation to an outgoing tenant for any fruit-trees or bushes or other improvement, he shall have the same rights as to compensation or removal as he would have had under this Act if the fruit-trees or bushes had been provided and planted or the improvement had been made by him and at his expense.

**6.**—(1) The compensation under the foregoing provisions of this Act, and such further compensation (if any) as is recoverable under the contract of tenancy shall, in default of agreement, be determined by a valuation made by a person appointed in default of agreement by the judge of the county court having jurisdiction in the place where the land is situated, on an application in writing being made for the purpose by the landlord or tenant, and, if not paid within fourteen days after the amount is agreed or determined, shall be recoverable upon order made by the county court as money ordered to be paid by a county court under its ordinary jurisdiction, is recoverable.

(2) The proper charges of the valuer for the valuation shall be borne by the landlord and tenant in such proportion as the

valuer shall direct, but be recoverable by the valuer from either of the parties and any amount paid by either of the parties in excess of the amount (if any) directed by the valuer to be borne by him shall be recoverable from the other party and may be deducted from any compensation payable to such party.

7. The foregoing provisions of this Act shall not apply to any land of which possession was taken by or on behalf of any Government department under the enactments relating to the Defence of the Realm or the regulations made thereunder and possession of which has been continued by virtue of any enactment, or to any land forming part of a royal park; but, save as aforesaid, the foregoing provisions of this Act shall apply to land vested in His Majesty in right of the Crown or the Duchy of Lancaster, and to land forming part of the possessions of the Duchy of Cornwall, and, except as otherwise hereinbefore expressly provided, to land vested in any Government department for public purposes.

8.—(1) The period during which an order for the compulsory acquisition of land for allotments is, under section one of the Land Settlement (Facilities) Act, 1919, exempted from the requirement of submission to and confirmation by the Minister is hereby extended to the thirty-first day of December, nineteen hundred and twenty-two.

(2) The restrictions imposed by section forty-one of the Small Holdings and Allotments Act, 1908, on the compulsory acquisition of land which has been acquired by any corporation or company for the purposes of a railway, dock, canal, water, or other public undertaking shall not apply to the hiring of land by a council of a borough or urban district or by the council of a county to whom the powers and duties of a borough or urban district council have been transferred under the provisions of subsection (2) of section twenty-four of the Small Holdings and Allotments Act, 1908, for the purpose of providing allotment gardens:

Provided that every such hiring shall be subject to a condition enabling—

(a) the corporation or company to resume possession of the land when required by the corporation or company for the purpose (not being the use of land for agriculture) for which it was acquired by the corporation or company; and

(b) nothing in this subsection shall prejudice the protection given by the said section forty-one to land which is the property of a local authority.

(3) Notwithstanding anything contained in any other enactment, counsel shall not be heard in any arbitration under this Act or as to compensation payable for land acquired

for allotments under the Allotments Acts unless the Minister otherwise directs.

(4) No land shall be authorized by an order under the Allotments Acts to be hired compulsorily for the purposes of allotments which at the date of the order is pasture land if it is proved to the satisfaction of the Minister that arable land which is equally suitable for the purpose of allotments to the pasture land proposed to be compulsorily hired is reasonably available for hiring by the council.

(5) Paragraph 2 (*b*) of Part II of Schedule I to the Small Holdings and Allotments Act, 1908 (which restricts the breaking up of pasture compulsorily hired) shall not apply to land compulsorily hired for the provision of allotment gardens.

**9.** The provisions of the Small Holdings and Allotments Acts, 1908 to 1919, enabling grants of land to be made to a county council for the purposes of small holdings at fee farm and other rents, and authorizing a county council to covenant to pay any such rent, shall apply with the necessary adaptations to the acquisition of land by the council of a borough or urban district for the purpose of providing allotments.

**10.**—(1) The council of a borough or urban district, or the council of a county to whom the powers and duties of a borough or urban district council have been transferred under the provisions of subsection (2) of section twenty-four of the Small Holdings and Allotments Act, 1908, may, after giving such notice of intention to enter as is hereinafter provided—

(*a*) enter upon any land to which this section applies for the purpose of providing allotment gardens thereon ;

(*b*) adapt any such land for use for such purpose ;

(*c*) let any such land for use by the tenant as an allotment garden or to any association (being an association to which land may be let by the council under the Small Holdings and Allotments Acts, 1908 to 1919) for the purpose of sub-letting for such use, but so that any tenancy created by the council shall terminate at the date when the right of occupation of the council is terminated under this section ;

(*d*) on the termination of such occupation remove any erection or work of adaptation making good any injury to the land caused by such removal.

(2) Before entry under this section, the council shall give not less than fourteen days' notice in writing to the owner of the land, in such manner as notices may be given to an owner under the regulations for the time being applicable to compulsory hiring of land under the Allotments Acts.

(3) The right of occupation of the council may be terminated—

(*a*) by not less than six months' notice in writing to that effect given by the council to the owner in manner aforesaid, and expiring on or before the sixth day of April, or on or after the twenty-ninth day of September in any year; or

(b) by not less than two months' notice in writing given by the owner to the council in any case where the land is required for any purpose other than the use of the land for agriculture.

(4) A tenant to whom land is let by a council under this section and whose tenancy is terminated by the termination of the right of occupation of the council shall, unless otherwise agreed in the contract of tenancy, be entitled to recover from the council such compensation (if any) as would have been recoverable if his tenancy had been terminated by notice to quit given by the council, and have the same right to remove his crops as if the tenancy had been so terminated.

(5) Any person who is interested in any land on which entry is made by the council under this section, and who suffers any loss by reason of the exercise of the powers conferred by this section shall, if he makes a claim not later than one year after the termination of the right of occupation, be entitled to be paid by the council such amount or amounts by way of periodical payments or otherwise as may represent the loss, and such amount or amounts shall in default of agreement be determined by a valuation made by a person appointed, in default of agreement, by the Minister:

Provided that a periodical payment of compensation in the nature of rent shall not exceed the rental value of the land as defined by this section.

(6) This section applies to—

(a) land which at the date of the notice of intended entry is not the subject of a rateable occupation; or

(b) land of which at the date of the notice of intended entry the Minister is in possession by himself or any person deriving title under him under the provisions of section one of the Defence of the Realm (Acquisition of Land) Act, 1916, as explained by section thirty of the Land Settlement (Facilities) Act, 1919, and which when possession thereof was first taken under the Defence of the Realm Regulation was not the subject of a rateable occupation;

except land being the property of a local authority or land which has been acquired by any corporation or company for the purposes of a railway, dock, canal, water, or other public undertaking, or forming part of any metropolitan common within the meaning of the Metropolitan Commons Act, 1866, or any land which is subject, or might be made subject, to regulation under an order or scheme made in pursuance of the Inclosure Acts, 1845 to 1899, or under any local Act or otherwise, or land which is or forms part of any town or village green, or any area dedicated or appropriated as a public park garden, or pleasure ground, or for use for the purposes of public recreation, or land forming part of the New Forest' (as defined in the New Forest Act, 1877), or of the trust property to which the National Trust Act, 1907, applies.

(7) For the purposes of this section—

The expression "rental value" means the annual rent which a tenant might reasonably be expected to pay for the land if the land had continued in the same condition as at the date when entry was made under this section, or at the date when possession thereof was so first taken as aforesaid, as the case may be.

The expression "rateable occupation" means such occupation as would involve liability to payment of the poor rate or any rate leviable in like manner as the poor rate.

The expression "owner" includes the person who, but for the occupation of the council, would be entitled to the possession of the land.

**11.**—(1) Where land has been let to a local authority or to an association for the purpose of being sub-let for use as allotment gardens, or is occupied by a council under the powers of entry conferred by this Act, and the landlord, or the person who but for such occupation would be entitled to the possession of the land, proposes to resume possession of the land in accordance with the provisions of this Act for any particular purpose, notice in writing of the purpose for which resumption is required shall be given to the local authority or association.

(2) The local authority or association may, by a counter notice served within ten days after receipt of such notice on the person requiring possession, demand that the question as to whether resumption of possession is required in good faith for the purpose specified in the notice shall be determined by arbitration under and in accordance with the provisions of the Second Schedule to the Agricultural Holdings Act, 1908.

(3) Possession of the land shall not be resumed until after the expiration of the said period of ten days or the determination of such question as aforesaid where such determination is demanded under this section.

(4) This section shall not apply to any case where resumption of possession is required by a corporation or company being the owners or lessees of a railway, dock, canal, water, or other public undertaking.

**12.**—(1) Where an order has been made for the compulsory acquisition of any land and notice to treat thereunder is not served by the acquiring authority within three calendar months after the date of the said order, or where confirmation of the said order is necessary, then after the date of the confirmation thereof the order so far as it relates to land in respect of which notice to treat has not been so served shall become null and void.

(2) Where an order has so become null and void as respects any land, no order authorizing the compulsory acquisition of that land or any part of such land shall, if made within three years after the expiration of the said three calendar months, be valid, unless confirmed by the Minister, or be so confirmed, unless it is proved to the satisfaction of the Minister that there are special reasons justifying the failure to exercise the powers under the original order and the making of the order submitted for confirmation.

**13.** The obligation of a council of a borough or urban district under the Allotments Acts to provide allotments shall, if the population thereof is ten thousand or upwards, be limited to the provision of allotment gardens not exceeding twenty poles in extent.

**14.**—(1) The council of every borough or urban district with a population of ten thousand or upwards shall, unless exempted by the Minister, after consultation with the Minister of Health, from the provisions of this section, establish an allotments committee, which may be an existing committee of the council or a sub-committee of an existing committee and all matters relating to the exercise and performance by the council of their powers and duties under the Allotments Acts as respects the provision of allotment gardens (except the power of raising a rate or borrowing money) shall stand referred to such committee, and the council before exercising any such powers shall, unless in their opinion the matter is urgent, receive and consider the report of the committee with respect to the matter in question, and the council may delegate to the committee, with or without restrictions, any of their said powers except as aforesaid.

(2) An allotments committee estabished under this section shall comprise persons, other than members of the council, being persons experienced in the management and cultivation of allotment gardens and representative of the interests of occupiers of allotment gardens in the borough or district, provided that the number of such representative members shall be not more than one-third of the total number of the members of the committee or be less than two or one-fifth of such total number whichever be the larger number.

(3) The accounts of any receipts or payments by or to a committee under powers delegated under this section shall be accounts of the council and made up and audited accordingly.

(4) In the case of a county borough, the council may appoint their small holdings committee, if constituted so as

to comply with the provisions of this section, to be their allotment committee under this section.

**15.** A county council may let land acquired or appropriated by the council for small holdings for cultivation as an allotment, or to a local authority or association, being an association to which land may be let by a council under the Small Holdings and Allotments Acts, 1908 to 1919, for the purpose of being sub-let for such use : Provided that this section shall not be deemed to authorize a council to let any land held by the council under a contract of tenancy or the use of any land so held in contravention of any term or condition of the contract.

**16.**—(1) A council shall not take any proceedings under the provisions of the Allotments Acts relating to allotments, unless in the opinion of the council the expenses of the council incurred under those provisions (other than such expenses as are hereinafter specified) may reasonably be expected, after the proceedings are taken, to be defrayed out of the receipts of the council under those provisions.

(2) For the purposes of this section, expenses and receipts shall be calculated in such manner as the Minister of Health may direct, and shall include expenses and receipts in respect of land acquired whether before or after the passing of this Act :

Provided that such expenses shall not include—

(a) expenses in relation to the acquisition of land other than the purchase price or rent, or other compensation payable in respect of the land ;
(b) expenses incurred in making roads to be used by the public ;
(c) sinking fund charges in respect of loans raised in connection with the purchase of land.

(3) Land let by a council under the Allotments Acts for use as an allotment shall be let at the full fair rent for such use and not more than a quarter's rent (except where the yearly rent is twenty shillings or less) shall be required to be paid in advance.

**17.**—(1) A council providing land for allotments whether under the Allotments Acts or otherwise may, by notice to the authority by which any rate is levied, require that the council shall be assessed to the rate as the occupiers of the land notwithstanding that the land or part thereof may be let, and in such case the council shall, for the purposes of any rate levied by that authority and made after the notice is given and before the notice is withdrawn, be deemed to be the occupiers of the land.

(2) The foregoing subsection shall apply to an association providing land for allotments in like manner as it applies to a

council, if at the request of the association the authority by which a rate is levied agrees that it shall so apply.

**18.**—(1) The maximum period for the repayment of money borrowed by the council of a borough or urban district or parish under the Allotments Acts shall, where the purpose for which the money is borrowed is the purchase of land for allotments, be eighty years, and the provisions of subsection (2) of section fifty-two of the Small Holdings and Allotments Act, 1908, relating to loans by the Public Works Loan Commissioners for small holdings shall extend to money borrowed by any such council for the purpose of providing allotments.

(2) Money borrowed by a council for the purpose of providing allotments shall not be reckoned as part of the total debt of the council for the purpose of any enactment limiting the powers of borrowing by the council.

**19.**—(1) Any person who by any act done without lawful authority or by negligence causes damage to any allotment garden or any crops or fences or buildings thereon shall be liable on summary conviction to a penalty not exceeding five pounds, but this provision shall not apply unless notice of this provision is conspicuously displayed on or near the allotment garden.

(2) Subsection (4) of section twenty-one of the Land Settlement (Facilities) Act, 1919, is hereby repealed.

**20.** If it appears to the Minister, in relation to the London County Council or the council of any county borough or Metropolitan borough, after holding a local inquiry at which the council, and such other persons as the person holding the inquiry, may, in his discretion, think fit to allow, shall be permitted to appear and be heard, that the council have failed to satisfy to the extent to which it is reasonably practicable, having regard to the provisions of the Allotments Acts, the demand for allotment gardens to be provided by the council the Minister may, by order, transfer to the Small Holdings Commissioners all or any of the powers of the council relating to the provision of allotment gardens and the provisions of section twenty-four of the Small Holdings and Allotments Act, 1908, shall apply as if references to the Commissioners were substituted for references to the county council and with such other adaptations as may be made by the order.

**21.**—(1) Notwithstanding anything in any other Act, the Commissioners of Woods may let for any term to a local authority under the Allotments Acts, and the local authority may take for the purpose of providing allotment gardens any land in the Forest (as defined in the New Forest Act, 1877) which is vested in His Majesty and was on the fifth day of April, nineteen hundred and twenty-two, being used for the provision of allotment gardens, and, with the consent of the Minister, such further land in the forest not exceeding sixty acres, as may be agreed between the Commissioners of Woods and the Verderers of the Forest:

Provided that, if at any time any land so let is used for any purpose other than the provision of allotment gardens, the lease shall become void and the land shall revert to His Majesty and be held in the same manner as it was held before its use for the provision of allotment gardens and subject to the same rights and liabilities so far as practicable.

(2) While a lease under this section has effect any land let thereunder shall be free from all rights of common and all other similar rights and privileges except the right of the public to use any highway on the land.

(3) Any rent received by the Commissioners under the lease shall be divisible between the Commissioners and the Verderers of the Forest in such proportions as may be agreed, or, in default of agreement, may be determined by the arbitration of a single arbitrator under the Arbitration Act, 1889, and the proportion received by the Verderers shall be applied as money received by the Verderers under the New Forest Act, 1877.

(4) Any inclosure under the Poor Relief Act, 1831, or any amending Act, of land in the forest made after the passing of this Act shall be void.

22.—(1) For the purposes of this Act, where the context permits—

 The expression "allotment garden" means an allotment not exceeding forty poles in extent which is wholly or mainly cultivated by the occupier for the production of vegetable or fruit crops for consumption by himself or his family;

 The expression "landlord" means in relation to any land the person for the time being entitled to receive the rents and profits of the land;

 The designations of landlord and tenant shall continue to apply to the parties until the conclusion of any proceedings taken under this Act in respect of compensation and shall include the legal personal representative of either party;

 The expression "council" shall, in the case of a rural parish not having a parish council, mean the parish meeting;

 The expression "industrial purpose" shall not include use for agriculture or sport, and the expression "agriculture" includes forestry, horticulture, or the keeping and breeding of livestock;

 The expression "the Allotments Acts" means the provisions of the Small Holdings and Allotments Acts, 1908 to 1919, which relate to allotments and this Act;

The expression "Minister" means the Minister of Agriculture and Fisheries;

The expression "borough" includes a metropolitan borough;

The expression "sinking fund charges" includes any charges for the repayment of loans whether by means of a sinking fund or otherwise.

(2) For the purposes of this Act, references to population shall be construed as references to population according to the published returns of the last census for the time being.

(3) Compensation recoverable by a tenant under this Act for crops or other things shall be based on the value thereof to an incoming tenant.

(4) Where land is used by the tenant thereof as an allotment garden, then, for the purposes of this Act, unless the contrary is proved—
  (a) the land shall be deemed to have been let to him to be used by him as an allotment garden; and
  (b) where the land has been sublet to him by a local authority or association which holds the land under a contract of tenancy, the land shall be deemed to have been let to that authority or association for the purpose of being sub-let for such use as aforesaid.

(5) The powers conferred by this Act on a council of a borough, may, in London, be exercised by the London County Council.

(6) For removing doubts, it is hereby declared that the expression "holding" in the Agricultural Holdings Act, 1908, and in the Agricultural Land Sales (Restriction of Notices to Quit) Act, 1919, does not include any allotment garden or any land cultivated as a garden unless it is cultivated wholly or mainly for the purpose of the trade or business of market gardening.

**23.**—(1) This Act may be cited as the Allotments Act, 1922, and the provisions of the Small Holdings and Allotments Acts, 1908 to 1919, which relate to allotments and this Act may be cited together as the Allotments Acts, 1908 to 1922.

(2) The enactments mentioned in the Schedule to this Act are hereby repealed to the extent specified in the third column of that schedule.

(3) This Act shall not apply to Scotland or Ireland.

## SCHEDULE.

Enactments Repealed (section 23.)

| Session and Chapter. | Short Title. | Extent of Repeal. |
|---|---|---|
| 8 & 9 Vict. c. 118. | The Inclosure Act, 1845. | In section one hundred and ten from "Provided" to the end of the section. |
| 50 & 51 Vict. c. 26. | The Allotments and Cottage Gardens Compensation for Crops Act, 1887. | The whole Act. |
| 53 & 54 Vict. c. 57. | The Tenants' Compensation Act, 1890. | The whole Act. |
| 8 Edw. 7, c. 36. | The Small Holdings and Allotments Act 1908. | Subsection (3) of section twenty-five. Subsection (1) of section twenty-seven, in section thirty the proviso to subsection (2). |
| 10 & 11 Geo. 5, c. 76. | The Agriculture Act, 1920. | Section eleven. |

(IV)

## ACQUISITION OF LAND (ASSESSMENT OF COMPENSATION) ACT, 1919.

(9 & 10 Geo. 5, Ch. 57.)

**(19th August, 1919.)**

(So far as it affects the acquisition of land for allotments in England and Wales.)

Be it enacted, etc. :—

1.—*Tribunal for Assessing Compensation in Respect of Land Compulsorily Acquired for Public Purposes.* (1) Where by or under any statute (whether passed before or after the passing of this Act) land is authorized to be acquired compulsorily by any Government Department or any local or public authority, any question of disputed compensation, and, where any part of the land to be acquired is subject to a lease which comprises land not acquired, any question as to the apportionment of the rent payable under the lease, shall be referred to and determined by the arbitration of such one of a panel of official arbitrators to be appointed under this section as may be selected in accordance with rules made by the Reference Committee under this section.

(2) Such number of persons, being persons with special knowledge in the valuation of land, as may be appointed for England and Wales, Scotland and Ireland by the Reference Committee, shall form a panel of persons to act as official arbitrators for the purposes of this Act in England and Wales, Scotland and Ireland respectively: Provided that of the members of the said panel for England and Wales one at least shall be a person having special knowledge of the valuation of land in Wales and acquainted with the Welsh language.

(3) A person appointed to be a member of the panel of official arbitrators shall hold office for such term certain as may be determined by the Treasury before his appointment, and whilst holding office shall not himself engage, or be a partner of any other person who engages, in private practice or business.

(4) There shall be paid out of moneys provided by Parliament to official arbitrators such salaries or remuneration as the Treasury may determine.

(5) The Reference Committee—
 (a) For England and Wales shall consist of the Lord Chief Justice of England, the Master of the Rolls and the President of the Surveyors' Institution.

2.—*Rules for the Assessment of Compensation.* In assessing compensation, an official arbitrator shall act in accordance with the following rules:—
 (1) No allowance shall be made on account of the acquisition being compulsory:
 (2) The value of land shall, subject as hereinafter provided, be taken to be the amount which the land if sold in the open market by a willing seller might be expected to realize: Provided always that the arbitrator shall be entitled to consider all returns and assessments of capital value for taxation made or acquiesced in by the claimant:
 (3) The special suitability or adaptability of the land for any purpose shall not be taken into account if that purpose is a purpose to which it could be applied only in pursuance of statutory powers, or for which there is no market apart from the special needs of a particular purchaser or the requirements of any Government Department or any local or public authority: Provided that any *bona fide* offer for

the purchase of the land made before the passing of this Act which may be brought to the notice of the arbitrator shall be taken into consideration :

(4) Where the value of the land is increased by reason of the use thereof or of any premises thereon in a manner which could be restrained by any court, or is contrary to law, or is detrimental to the health of the inmates of the premises or to the public health, the amount of that increase shall not be taken into account :

(5) Where land is, and but for the compulsory acquisition would continue to be, devoted to a purpose of such a nature that there is no general demand or market for land for that purpose, the compensation may, if the official arbitrator is satisfied that reinstatement in some other place is *bona fide* intended, be assessed on the basis of the reasonable cost of equivalent reinstatement :

(6) The provisions of Rule (2) shall not affect the assessment of compensation for disturbance or any other matter not directly based on the value of land.

For the purposes of this section, an official arbitrator shall be entitled to be furnished with such returns and assessments as he may require.

3.—*Provision as to Procedure before Official Arbitrators.*

(1) In any proceedings before an official arbitrator, not more than one expert witness on either side shall be heard unless the official arbitrator otherwise directs :

Provided that, where the claim includes a claim for compensation in respect of minerals, or disturbance of business, as well as in respect of land, one additional expert witness on either side on the value of the minerals, or, as the case may be, on the damage suffered by reason of the disturbance may be allowed.

(2) It shall not be necessary for an official arbitrator to make any declaration before entering into the consideration of any matter referred to him.

(3) The official arbitrator shall, on the application of either party, specify the amount awarded in respect of any particular matter the subject of the award.

(4) The official arbitrator shall be entitled to enter on and inspect any land which is the subject of proceedings before him.

(5) Proceedings under this Act shall be heard by an official arbitrator sitting in public.

(6) The fees to be charged in respect of proceedings before official arbitrators shall be such as the Treasury may prescribe.

(7) Subject as aforesaid, the Reference Committee may make rules regulating the procedure before official arbitrators.

4.—*Consolidation of Proceedings on Claims for Compensation in Respect of Various Interests in the Same Land.* Where notices to treat have been served for the acquisition of the several interests in the land to be acquired, the claims of the persons entitled to such interests shall, so far as practicable, and so far as not agreed and if the acquiring authority so desire, be heard and determined by the same official arbitrator, and the Reference Committee may make rules providing that such claims shall be heard together, but the value of the several interests in the land having a market value shall be separately assessed.

5.—*Provisions as to Costs.* (1) Where the acquiring authority has made an unconditional offer in writing of any sum as compensation to any claimant and the sum awarded by an official arbitrator to that claimant does not exceed the sum offered, the official arbitrator shall, unless for special reasons he thinks proper not to do so, order the claimant to bear his own costs and to pay the costs of the acquiring authority so far as such costs were incurred after the offer was made.

(2) If the official arbitrator is satisfied that a claimant has failed to deliver to the acquiring authority a notice in writing of the amount claimed by him giving sufficient particulars and in sufficient time to enable the acquiring authority to make a proper offer the foregoing provisions of this section shall apply as if an unconditional offer had been made by the acquiring authority at the time when in the opinion of the official arbitrator sufficient particulars should have been furnished and the claimant had been awarded a sum not exceeding the amount of such offer.

The notice of claim shall state the exact nature of the interest in respect of which compensation is claimed, and give details of the compensation claimed, distinguishing the amounts under separate heads and showing how the amount claimed under each head is calculated, and when such a notice of claim has been delivered the acquiring authority may, at any time within six weeks after the delivery thereof, withdraw any notice to treat which has been served on the claimant or on any other person interested in the land authorized to be acquired, but shall be liable to pay compensation to any such claimant or other person for any loss or expenses occasioned by the notice to treat having been given to him and withdrawn, and the amount of such compensation shall, in default of agreement, be determined by an official arbitrator.

(3) Where a claimant has made an unconditional offer in writing to accept any sum as compensation and has complied with the provisions of the last preceding subsection, and the sum awarded is equal to or exceeds that sum, the official arbitrator shall, unless for special reasons he thinks proper

not to do so, order the acquiring authority to bear their own costs and to pay the costs of the claimant so far as such costs were incurred after the offer was made.

(4) Subject as aforesaid, the costs of an arbitration under this Act shall be in the discretion of the official arbitrator who may direct to and by whom and in what manner those costs or any part thereof shall be paid, and the official arbitrator may in any case disallow the cost of counsel.

(5) An official arbitrator may himself tax the amount of costs ordered to be paid, or may direct in what manner they are to be taxed.

(6) Where an official arbitrator orders the claimant to pay the costs, or any part of the costs, of the acquiring authority, the acquiring authority may deduct the amount so payable by the claimant from the amount of the compensation payable to him.

(7) Without prejudice to any other method of recovery, the amount of costs ordered to be paid by a claimant, or such part thereof as is not covered by such deduction as aforesaid shall be recoverable from him by the acquiring authority summarily as a civil debt.

(8) For the purpose of this section, costs include any fees, charges, and expenses of the arbitration or award.

6.—*Finality of Award and Statement of Special Cases.* (1) The decision of an official arbitrator upon any question of fact, shall be final and binding on the parties, and the persons claiming under them respectively, but the official arbitrator may, and shall, if the High Court so directs, state at any stage of the proceedings, in the form of a special case for the opinion of the High Court, any question of law arising in the course of the proceedings, and may state his award as to the whole or part thereof in the form of a special case for the opinion of the High Court.

(2) The decision of the High Court upon any case so stated shall be final and conclusive, and shall not be subject to appeal to any other court.

7 —*Effect of Act on Existing Enactments.* (1) The provisions of the Act or order by which the land is authorized to be acquired, or of any Act incorporated therewith, shall, in relation to the matters dealt with in this Act, have effect subject to this Act, and so far as inconsistent with this Act those provisions shall cease to have or shall not have effect:

Provided that nothing in this Act relating to the rules for assessing compensation shall affect any special provisions as to the assessment of the value of land acquired for the purposes of Part I or Part II of the Housing of the Working Classes Act, 1890, or under the Defence of the Realm (Acquisition of Land) Act, 1916, and contained in those Acts respectively, or any Act amending those Acts, if and so far as the provisions in those Acts are inconsistent with the rules under this Act and the provisions of the Second Schedule to the Housing of the Working Classes Act, 1890, as amended by any subsequent enactment (except paragraphs (4), (5), (29), and (31) thereof) shall apply to an official arbitrator as they apply to an arbitrator appointed under that schedule, and an official arbitrator may exercise all the powers conferred by those provisions on such arbitrator.

(2) The provisions of this Act shall apply to the determination of the amount of rent or compensation payable in respect of land authorized to be hired compulsorily under the Small Holdings and Allotments Act, 1908, or any Act amending that Act, and any matter required thereby to be determined by a valuer appointed by the Board of Agriculture and Fisheries shall be determined by an official arbitrator in accordance with this Act.

8.—*Power to Refer to Commissioners of Inland Revenue or to Agreed Arbitrator.* (1) Nothing in this Act shall prevent, if the parties so agree, the reference of any question as to disputed compensation or apportionment of rent to the Commissioners of Inland Revenue or to an arbitrator agreed on between the parties.

(2) Where a question is so referred to the Commissioners of Inland Revenue, the Commissioners shall not proceed by arbitration, but shall cause an assessment to be made in accordance with the rules for the assessment of compensation under this Act, and the following provisions shall have effect :—

(a) The parties shall comply with any direction or requirements as to the furnishing of information (whether orally or in writing) and the production of documents and otherwise ;

(b) Any officer of the Commissioners appointed for the purpose shall be entitled to enter on and inspect any land which is subject to the reference to them ;

(c) The Commissioners, if either party so desires within such time as the Commissioners may allow, shall give the parties an opportunity of being heard before such officer of the valuation office of the Commissioners as the Commissioners may appoint for the purpose ;

(d) The assessment when made shall be published to the parties and take effect as if it were an award of an official arbitrator under this Act ;

(e) If either party refuses or neglects to comply with any direction or requirement of the Commissioners, the Commissioners may decline to proceed with the matter, and in that case the question shall be referred to an official arbitrator as if there had been no reference to the Commissioners, and the official arbitrator, when awarding costs shall take into consideration any report of the Commissioners as to the refusal or neglect which rendered such a reference to him necessary.

(3) Where a question is referred to an arbitrator under subsection (1) of this section, the provisions of this Act, except sections one and four and so much of section three as requires proceedings to be in public and as provides for the fixing of fees, shall apply as if the arbitrator was an official arbitrator.

(4) Either party to a claim for compensation may require the Commissioners for Inland Revenue to assess the value of the land in respect of which the claim arises, and a copy of any such assessment shall be sent forthwith by the Commissioners to the other party, and a certified copy of such assessment shall be admissible in evidence of that value in proceedings before the official arbitrator, and the officer who made the assessment shall attend, if the official arbitrator so require, to answer such questions as the official arbitrator may think fit to put to him thereon.

9.—*Certificates of Value of Official Arbitrators.* An official arbitrator may on the application of any person certify the value of land being sold by him to a Government department or public or local authority, and the sale of the land to the department or authority at the price so certified shall be deemed to be a sale at the best price that can reasonably be obtained.

12.—*Short Title, Commencement and Interpretation.* (1) This Act may be cited as the Acquisition of Land (Assessment of Compensation) Act, 1919, and shall come into operation on the first day of September nineteen hundred and nineteen, but shall not apply to the determination of any question where before that date the appointment of an arbitration, valuation or other tribunal to determine the question has been completed, or a jury has been empanelled for the purpose.

(2) For the purposes of this Act, the expression " land " includes water and any interests in land or water and any easement or right in, to, or over land or water, and " public authority " means any body of persons, not trading for profit, authorized by or under any Act to carry on a railway, canal, dock, water or other public undertaking.

## (V)

### AGRICULTURE ACT, 1920.

(10 & 11 Geo. 5, Ch. 76), 23rd December, 1920.

(So far as allotments may be affected.)

**10.**—(1) Where the tenancy of a holding terminates after the commencement of this Act by reason of a notice to quit given, after the twentieth day of May, nineteen hundred and twenty, by the landlord, and in consequence of such notice the tenant quits the holding, then, unless the tenant—

(a) Was not at the date of the notice cultivating the holding according to the rules of good husbandry; or

(b) Had at the date of the notice, failed to comply within a reasonable time with any notice in writing by the landlord served on him requiring him to pay any rent due in respect of the holding or to remedy any breach being a breach which was capable of being remedied of any term or condition of the tenancy consistent with good husbandry; or

(c) Had, at the date of the notice, materially prejudiced the interests of the landlord by committing a breach which was not capable of being remedied of any term or condition of the tenancy consistent with good husbandry; or

(d) Was at the date of the notice a person who had become bankrupt or compounded with his creditors; or

(e) Has, after the commencement of this Act, refused, or within a reasonable time failed, to agree to a demand made to him in writing by the landlord for arbitration as to the rent to be paid for the holding as from the next ensuing date at which the tenancy could have been terminated by notice to quit given by the landlord at the date of the said demand; or

(f) Had, at the date of the notice, unreasonably refused, or within a reasonable time failed, to comply with a demand made to him in writing by the landlord requiring him to execute at the expense of the landlord an agreement setting out the existing terms of the tenancy;

and, in the case of a notice to quit given after the commencement of this Act, unless the notice to quit states that it is given for one or more of the reasons aforesaid, compensation for the disturbance shall be payable by the landlord to the tenant in accordance with the provisions of this section:

Provided that compensation shall not be payable under

this section in any case where the landlord has made to the tenant an offer in writing to withdraw the notice to quit and the tenant has unreasonably refused or failed to accept the offer.

(2) The landlord of a holding may at any time apply to the agricultural committee for the area in which the holding is situate for a certificate that the tenant is not cultivating the holding according to the rules of good husbandry, and, on any such application being made, the committee, after giving to the landlord and the tenant or their respective representatives an opportunity of being heard, shall, as they think proper, either grant or refuse the certificate within one month after the date of the application.

The landlord or tenant may, within seven days after the notification to him of the refusal or grant by the committee of a certificate, require the question as to whether the holding is being cultivated according to the rules of good husbandry to be referred to an arbitrator who may grant a certificate for the purpose of this subsection or revoke the certificate granted by the committee, and the award of the arbitrator shall be given within twenty-eight days of the date on which the matter is referred to him.

Subject to any such appeal, a certificate granted under this subsection shall be conclusive evidence that the holding is not being cultivated according to the rules of good husbandry.

In the case of a holding situate in a county borough for which an agricultural committee has not been appointed, this subsection shall have effect with the substitution of the Minister for an agricultural committee.

(3) Where, after the commencement of this Act the landlord of a holding refuses, or within a reasonable time fails to agree to, a demand made to him in writing by the tenant for arbitration as to the rent to be paid for the holding as from the next ensuing date at which the tenancy could have been terminated by notice to quit given by the tenant at the date of the said demand, and by reason of the refusal or failure the tenant exercises his power of terminating the tenancy by a notice stating that it is given for that reason, the tenant shall be entitled to compensation in the same manner as if the tenancy had been terminated by notice to quit given by the landlord. Provided that such compensation shall not be payable if the circumstances are such that a notice to quit could have been given by the landlord for any of the reasons mentioned in paragraphs (a), (b), or (c) of subsection (1) of this section.

(4) The provisions of this section relating to demands for arbitration as to the rent to be paid for a holding shall not apply where the demand, if made later than six months after the commencement of this Act, is so made that the increase or

reduction of the rent would take effect at some time before the expiration of two years from the commencement of the tenancy of the holding or from the date on which a previous increase or reduction of the rent took effect.

(5) An arbitrator, in determining for the purposes of this section what rent is properly payable in respect of a holding shall not take into account any increase in the rental value which is due to improvements which have been executed thereon so far as they were executed wholly or partly by and at the expense of the tenant without any equivalent allowance or benefit made or given by the landlord in consideration of their execution, and have not been executed by him under an obligation imposed by the terms of his contract of tenancy, or fix the rent at a higher amount than would have been properly payable if those improvements had not been so executed, and shall not fix the rent at a lower amount by reason of any dilapidation or deterioration of land or buildings made or permitted by the tenant.

(6) The compensation payable under this section shall be a sum representing such loss or expense directly attributable to the quitting of the holding as the tenant may unavoidably incur upon or in connection with the sale or removal of his household goods, implements of husbandry, fixtures, farm produce or farm stock on or used in connection with the holding, and shall include any expenses reasonably incurred by him in the preparation of his claim for compensation (not being costs of an arbitration to determine the amount of the compensation), but for the avoidance of disputes such sum shall, for the purposes of this Act, be computed at an amount equal to one year's rent of the holding, unless it is proved that the loss and expenses so incurred exceed an amount equal to one year's rent of the holding, in which case the sum recoverable shall be such as represents the whole loss and expenses so incurred up to a maximum amount equal to two years' rent of the holding.

(7) Compensation shall not be payable under this section—
(a) In respect of the sale of any goods, implements, fixtures, produce, or stock unless the tenant has before the sale given the landlord a reasonable opportunity of making a valuation thereof ; or
(b) Unless the tenant has, not less than one month before the termination of the tenancy, given notice in writing to the landlord of his intention to make a claim for compensation under this section ; or
(c) Where the tenant with whom the contract of tenancy was made has died within three months before the date of the notice to quit ; or
(d) If in a case in which the tenant under section twenty-three of the Act of 1908 accepts a notice to quit

part of his holding as a notice to quit the entire holding, the part of the holding affected by the notice given by the landlord, together with any other part of the holding affected by any previous notice given under that section by the landlord to the tenant, is less than one-fourth part of the original holding, or the holding as proposed to be diminished is reasonably capable of being cultivated as a separate holding, except compensation in respect of the part of the holding to which the notice to quit related ; or

(e) Where the holding was let to the tenant by a corporation carrying on a railway, dock, canal, water, or other undertaking, or by a Government Department, or a local authority, and possession of the holding is required by the corporation, department, or authority for the purpose (not being the use of the land for agriculture) for which it was acquired by the corporation, department, or authority, or appropriated under any statutory provision ; or

(f) In the case of a permanent pasture which the landlord has been in the habit of letting annually for seasonal grazing, and which has since the fourth day of August, nineteen hundred and fourteen, and before the commencement of this Act, been let to a tenant for a definite and limited period for cultivation as arable land, on the condition that the tenant shall, along with the last or waygoing crop, sow permanent grass seeds ; or

(g) Where a written contract of tenancy has been entered into (whether before or after the commencement of this Act) for the letting by the landlord to the tenant of a holding, which at the time of the creation of the tenancy had then been for a period of not less than twelve months in the occupation of the landlord, upon the express terms that if the landlord desires to resume that occupation before the expiration of a specified term not exceeding seven years the landlord should be entitled to give notice to quit without becoming liable to pay to the tenant any compensation for disturbance, and the landlord desires to resume occupation within the specified period, and such notice to quit has been given accordingly.

(8) In any case, where a tenant holds two or more holdings, whether from the same landlord or different landlords, and receives notice to quit, one or more, but not all of the holdings, the compensation for disturbance in respect of the holding or holdings shall be reduced by such amount as is shown to the

satisfaction of the arbitrator to represent the reduction (if any) of the loss attributable to the notice to quit by reason of the continuance in possession by the tenant of the other holding or holdings.

(9) The landlord shall, on an application made in writing after the commencement of this Act by the tenant of a holding to whom a notice to quit has been given which does not state the reasons for which it is given, furnish to the tenant within twenty-eight days after the receipt of the application a statement in writing of the reasons for the giving of the notice, and, if he fails unreasonably so to do, compensation shall be payable under this section as if the notice to quit had not been given for a reason specified in subsection (1) of this section.

(10) If any question arises as to whether compensation is payable under this section or as to the amount payable by way of compensation under this section, the question shall, in default of agreement, be determined by arbitration under the Act of 1908.

(11) The expression "holding" in this section shall not include any land which forms part of any park, garden, or pleasure ground attached to and usually occupied with the mansion house, or any land adjoining the mansion house which is required for its protection or amenity, and the compensation for disturbance payable in respect of a notice to quit given in respect of any such land shall be such compensation (if any) as would have been payable under section eleven of the Act of 1908 if this Act had not been passed.

(12) Compensation payable under this section shall be in addition to any compensation to which the tenant may be entitled in respect of improvements, and shall be recoverable in the same manner as such compensation and be payable notwithstanding any agreement to the contrary.

\* \* \* \* \*

**28.**—(1) Notwithstanding any provision in a contract of tenancy to the contrary, a notice to quit a holding shall be invalid if it purports to terminate the tenancy before the expiration of twelve months from the end of the then current year of tenancy; but nothing in this section shall extend to a case where a receiving order in bankruptcy is made against the tenant.

(2) Section twenty-two of the Act of 1908 (which relates to the time of notices to quit), is hereby repealed.

(3) This section shall not apply to—
   (a) Any notice given by or on behalf of the Admiralty, War Department, or Air Council under the provisions of any agreement of tenancy where possession of the land is required for naval, military, or air force purposes; or

(b) Any notice given by a corporation carrying on a railway, dock, canal, water, or other undertaking in respect of any land acquired by the corporation for the purposes of their undertaking or by a government department or local authority where possession of the land is required by the corporation, government department or authority for the purpose (not being the use of the land for agriculture) for which it was acquired by the corporation, department, or authority or appropriated under any statutory provision ; or

(c) Any notice given in pursuance of a provision in the contract of tenancy authorizing the resumption of possession of the holding or some part thereof for some specified purpose, unless that purpose is the use of the land for agriculture ; or

(d) Any notice given by a tenant to a sub-tenant ; or

(e) Any notice given before the commencement of this Act.

\* \* \* \* \*

**33.**—In this Act, unless the context otherwise requires—

(1) The expression " the Minister " means the Minister of Agriculture and Fisheries.

\* \* \* \* \*

(4) The expression "rules of good husbandry" means (due regard being had to the character of the holding) so far as is practicable having regard to its character and position—

(a) The maintenance of the land (whether arable, meadow, or pasture), clean and in a good state of cultivation and fertility, and in good condition ; and

(b) The maintenance and clearing of drains, embankments, and ditches ; and

(c) The maintenance and proper repair of fences, stone walls, gates, and hedges ; and

(d) The execution of repairs to buildings, being repairs which are necessary for the proper cultivation and working of the land on which they are to be executed ; and

(e) Such rules of good husbandry as are generally recognized as applying to holdings of the same character and in the same neighbourhood as the holding in respect of which the expression is to be applied :

Provided that the foregoing definition shall not imply an obligation on the part of any person to maintain or clear drains, embankments, or ditches, if and so far as the execution of the works required is rendered impossible (except at prohibitive or unreasonable expense) by reason of subsidence of any land or the blocking of outfalls which are not under the control of that person, or in its application to land in the

occupation of a tenant imply an obligation on the part of the tenant—
  (i) To maintain or clear drains, embankments, or ditches, or to maintain or properly repair fences, stone walls, gates, or hedges where such work is not required to be done by him under his contract or tenancy ; or
  (ii) To execute repairs to buildings which are not required to be executed by him under his contract of tenancy :

(5) The expression "the Act of 1908" means the Agricultural Holdings Act, 1908, and the expression "the Act of 1917" means the Corn Production Act, 1917.

\* \* \* \* \*

**36.**—(1) This Act shall come into operation on the first day of January, nineteen hundred and twenty-one.

\* \* \* \* \*

(VI)

**THE SMALL HOLDINGS AND ALLOTMENTS (COMPULSORY PURCHASE) REGULATIONS, 1922 (dated 26th September, 1922).**

MADE BY THE MINISTER OF AGRICULTURE AND FISHERIES UNDER THE SMALL HOLDINGS AND ALLOTMENTS ACTS, 1908 TO 1919, AND THE ALLOTMENTS ACT, 1922.

The Minister of Agriculture and Fisheries in pursuance of the provisions of the Small Holdings and Allotments Acts, 1908 to 1919, and the Allotments Act, 1922, hereby makes the following Regulations :—

*Orders for Compulsory Purchase.*

1. A Compulsory Order for purchase made by a Council shall be in the form set forth in the Appendix to these Regulations or to the like effect ; Provided that an Order if submitted to the Minister of Agriculture and Fisheries (in these Regulations referred to as "the Minister") for confirmation may be modified by the Minister after notice of the intended modification to the Council and to those persons interested in the land who, in the opinion of the Minister, would be affected thereby, and after consideration of any objection thereto presented to the Minister within the time prescribed by such notice.

2. Notice of the making of an Order for compulsory purchase to which Section one of the Land Settlement (Facilities) Act, 1919, as amended by section 8 (1) of the Allotments Act, 1922, applies shall be given as soon as practicable to each owner, lessee and occupier of the land authorized to be acquired. The notice shall be accompanied by a copy of the Order (except any plan annexed or referred to therein) and shall state the place where a copy of any plan annexed or referred to in the Order can be obtained free of charge by any person interested in the land.

3.—(1) When a Council propose to purchase land compulsorily under an Order which requires confirmation by the Minister under the Small Holdings and Allotments Acts, 1908 to 1919, the Council, not less than one calendar month before they submit the Compulsory Order to the Minister, shall publish the Order by means of a notice, containing such particulars as are prescribed by this Regulation, inserted as an advertisement in one or more newspapers circulating in the locality, and by furnishing a copy of the Order (except any plan annexed to or referred to in the Order) free of charge to any person interested in the land who shall apply for the same. The Council shall also give notice of the Order, containing such particulars as are required by this Regulation, to the Minister and to each owner, lessee, and occupier of the land proposed to be purchased, or to such of them as shall be known to the Council.

(2) Every notice under this Regulation shall contain the following particulars :—
- (a) the purpose for which the land is proposed to be purchased ;
- (b) the quantity, description, and situation of the land and the names of the reputed owners, lessees, and occupiers thereof ;
- (c) the place where copies of the Order (except any plan annexed to or referred to in the Order) may be obtained free of charge by any person interested in the land ;
- (d) the place where the plan (if any) annexed to or referred to in the Order may at all reasonable times, until the Order is submitted to the Minister, be inspected by or on behalf of any person interested in the land.

(3) Every notice shall also state that any objection must be presented to the Minister, and every notice sent to an owner, lessee or occupier shall state the period within which an objection by him may be so presented in accordance with these Regulations. A notice may also state that a copy of every objection should be sent to the Clerk to the Council.

(4) If the Council is a County Council acting on behalf of a Parish Council or Parish Meeting the notice shall so state and give the name of the parish.

4. The period within which an objection to a Compulsory Order may, under the preceding Regulation, be presented to the Minister by a person interested in the land to which the Order relates shall be the period of one calendar month from and after the date on which notice of the Order is sent to him, or if no notice is sent to him in that case from and after the date of the latest advertisement of a notice of the Order.

5. Notice of the confirmation of the Order shall be given by the Council as soon as practicable to each owner, lessee, and occupier of the land authorized to be purchased, and a copy of the Order and of any plan annexed to or referred to in the Order shall be furnished by the Council to any person interested in the land on application by such person.

6.—(1) Every notice required to be given by the Council to an owner or other person interested in land proposed or authorized to be purchased, shall either be served personally on such person or sent by post to or left at his usual place of abode in the United Kingdom, if any such can after diligent inquiry be found, and in case any such person shall be absent from the United Kingdom or cannot be found after diligent inquiry, shall be sent by post to or left with any agent ordinarily receiving the rents of the land on behalf of such person, and a copy thereof shall also be sent by post to or left with the occupier of the land to which such notice relates, or, if there be no such occupier, shall be affixed upon some conspicuous part of such land.

(2) If an owner or other person interested be a corporation aggregate, such notice shall be sent by post to or left at the principal office of business of such corporation, or if no such office can after diligent inquiry be found, shall be sent by post to or served on some principal officer, if any, of such corporation.

7. Where a Council propose to purchase compulsorily the estate and interest of a lessee only, the Order shall so state, and these Regulations shall apply with the necessary modifications.

8. In these Regulations, unless the context otherwise requires—

"Owner" in relation to any land proposed or authorized to be purchased means the person who by himself or his agent is in actual possession, or receipt of the rents or profits, of the land (except a lessee) and that without regard to the real amount of interest of such person;

"Lessee" includes a tenant holding under an agreement for a lease;

"Compulsory Order" means an Order under the Small Holdings and Allotments Acts, 1908 to 1919, and the Allotments Act, 1922, which authorizes land to be compulsorily purchased;

"Land" includes stints and other alienable common rights of grazing.

9. These Regulations shall apply to a compulsory purchase by the Small Holdings Commissioners acting in default of a Council or by the Minister with the substitution of those Commissioners or the Minister, as the case may be, for the Council.

10. The Regulations as to compulsory purchase made by the Board of Agriculture and Fisheries on the 8th day of September, nineteen hundred and nineteen, are hereby revoked, but not so as to affect any Order made before the date of these Regulations.

11. These Regulations may be cited as the Small Holdings and Allotments (Compulsory Purchase) Regulations, 1922.

In witness whereof the Official Seal of the Minister of Agriculture and Fisheries is hereunto affixed this twenty-sixth day of September, nineteen hundred and twenty-two.

(L.S.)            H. L. FRENCH,

*Assistant Secretary.*

## APPENDIX.

1. The * are hereby empowered for the purpose of providing †· to put in force as respects the [several] land[s] described in the schedule hereto the provisions of the Lands Clauses Acts with respect to the purchase and taking of land otherwise than by agreement, but subject to the terms of the Small Holdings and Allotments Acts, 1908 to 1919,‡ and this Order.

2. This Order shall take effect as if it incorporated, subject to the necessary adaptations, the Lands Clauses Acts and sections seventy-seven to eighty-five of the Railways Clauses Consolidation Act, 1845, but subject to this modification, that any question of disputed compensation shall be determined under and in accordance with the provisions of the Acquisition of Land (Assessment of Compensation) Act, 1919, and the Small Holdings and Allotments Acts, 1908 to 1919.‡

[*Here insert any provision for the continuance of an existing easement or the creation of a new easement over the land(s).*]

3. Nothing in this Order as made or confirmed shall entitle the Council, except with the consent of the Minister of Agriculture and Fisheries, to require any party to sell or convey part only of [any of] the [several] land[s] described in the schedule hereto if such party is willing and able to sell and convey the whole thereof.

4. (*Where the Order applies to glebe land or other land belonging to an ecclesiastical benefice insert the following paragraph.*) Any sum agreed upon or awarded for the purchase of the land[s], or payable by way of compensation for the damage to be sustained by the owner by reason of severance or other injury affecting the land[s] shall not be paid as directed by the Lands Clauses Acts, but shall be paid to the Ecclesiastical Commissioners to be applied by them as money paid to them upon a sale under the Ecclesiastical Leasing Acts of land belonging to a benefice.

5. (*Where the Order relates to small holdings insert the following paragraph.*) The powers conferred by this Order shall cease after the expiration of one year from the date of confirmation of this Order by the Minister of Agriculture and Fisheries unless such period is extended by the Minister.

6. (*Where the Order relates to allotments or allotment gardens insert the following paragraph.*) The powers conferred by this Order shall cease after the expiration of three calendar months from the date hereof or from the date of confirmation by the

---

\* Insert " County Council of ," or " County Council of acting on behalf of the Parish Council " [*or* " Meeting "] or " Mayor, Aldermen, and Burgesses of the Borough of ," or " District Council."

† Insert " small holdings," or " allotments," or " allotment gardens," as the case may be.

‡ Insert here " and the Allotments Act, 1922," if the Order is made for the purpose of providing allotments or allotment gardens.

Minister of Agriculture and Fisheries if the Order is so confirmed.
Made by the * the day
of 19 . [Seal of the Council.]
*or*
Made on behalf of the * the day
of 19 , by their Small Holdings and Allotments Sub-
Committee. [Signature of Clerk to the Council.]

SCHEDULE TO FORM OR ORDER FOR COMPULSORY PURCHASE.

[Description of land[s] proposed or authorized to be purchased.]
If severally described, number consecutively.

(VII)

THE SMALL HOLDINGS AND ALLOTMENTS (COMPULSORY HIRING) REGULATIONS, 1922 (dated 26th September 1922).

MADE BY THE MINISTER OF AGRICULTURE AND FISHERIES UNDER THE SMALL HOLDINGS AND ALLOTMENTS ACTS, 1908 TO 1919, AND THE ALLOTMENTS ACT, 1922.

The Minister of Agriculture and Fisheries, in pursuance of the provisions of the Small Holdings and Allotments Acts, 1908 to 1919, and the Allotments Act, 1922, does hereby make the following Regulations :—

PART I.

*Orders for Compulsory Hiring.*

1. A Compulsory Order for hiring made by a Council shall be in the Form set forth in the Appendix to these Regulations or to the like effect; Provided that an Order if submitted to the Minister for confirmation may be modified by the Minister after notice of the intended modification to the Council and to those persons interested in the land who, in the opinion of the Minister, would be affected thereby, and after consideration of any objection thereto presented to the Minister within the time prescribed by such notice.

2. Notice of the making of an Order for compulsory hiring, to which Section one of the Land Settlement (Facilities) Act, 1919, as amended by Section 8 (1) of the Allotments Act, 1922, applies shall be given as soon as practicable to each owner, lessee and occupier of the land authorized to be acquired. The notice shall be accompanied by a copy of the Order (except any plan annexed or referred to therein) and shall state the place where a

---

* Insert " County Council of ," or " County Council of acting on behalf of the Parish Council " [*or* " Meeting "], or " Mayor, Aldermen, and Burgesses of the Borough of ," or " District Council."

COMPULSORY HIRING REGULATIONS 125

copy of any plan annexed or referred to in the Order can be obtained free of charge by any person interested in the land.

3.—(1) When a Council propose to hire land compulsorily under an Order which requires confirmation by the Minister under the Small Holdings and Allotments Acts, 1908 to 1919, the Council, not less than one calendar month before they submit the Order to the Minister, shall publish the Order by means of a notice containing such particulars as are prescribed by this Regulation, inserted as an advertisement in one or more newspapers circulating in the locality and by furnishing a copy of the Order (except any plan annexed to or referred to in the Order) free of charge to any person interested in the land who shall apply for the same. The Council shall also give notice of the Order containing such particulars as are required by this Regulation, to the Minister and to each owner, lessee, and occupier of the land proposed to be hired, or to such of them as shall be known to the Council.

(2) Every notice under this Regulation shall contain the following particulars :—
  (a) the purpose for which the land is proposed to be hired ;
  (b) the quantity, description, and situation of the land and the names of the reputed owners, lessees, and occupiers thereof ;
  (c) the number of years (with a part of a year, if so desired), for which the land is proposed to be hired ;
  (d) the place where copies of the Order (except any plan annexed to or referred to in the Order) may be obtained free of charge by any person interested in the land ;
  (e) the place where the plan (if any) annexed to or referred to in the Order may at all reasonable times until the Order is submitted to the Minister be inspected by or on behalf of any person interested in the land.

(3) Every notice shall also state that any objection must be presented to the Minister, and every notice sent to an owner, lessee or occupier shall state the period within which an objection may be so presented in accordance with these Regulations. A notice may also state that a copy of every objection should be sent to the Clerk to the Council.

(4) If the Council is a County Council acting on behalf of a Parish Council or Parish Meeting the notice shall so state and give the name of the parish.

4. The period within which an objection to a Compulsory Order may, under the preceding Regulation, be presented to the Minister by a person interested in the land to which the Order relates shall be the period of one calendar month from and after the date on which notice of the Order is sent to him, or if no notice is sent to him, in that case from and after the date of the latest advertisement of a notice of the Order.

5.—(1) Notice of the confirmation of the Order shall be given by the Council as soon as practicable to each owner, lessee, and occupier of the land authorized to be hired, and a copy of the Order, and of any plan annexed to or referred to in the Order, shall be furnished by the Council to any person interested in the land on application by such person.

(2) Upon the application of any person interested in the land

authorized to be hired, or in the interest of an existing tenant which will or may be extinguished by the compulsory hiring, the Order shall be so framed as to make such provision as is necessary for securing the interest of any party other than the owner or existing tenant in any compensation payable in respect of the compulsory hiring, and for that purpose there may be incorporated in the Order, with such adaptations as are required, any of the provisions of the Lands Clauses Consolidation Act, 1845, which relate to compensation coming to parties having limited interests.

PART II.

*Procedure for Enforcing Compulsory Hiring Order.*

6.—(1) When the Council require to hire compulsorily any land authorized to be hired by a Compulsory Order, they shall give notice to that effect to the owner of such land, and to any existing tenant thereof, or to such of the said parties as shall, after diligent inquiry, be known to the Council, and by such notice shall demand from such parties the particulars of their estate and interest in such land, in so far as such particulars are required in order to ascertain the owner thereof and the interests of the existing tenants (if any) ; and every such notice shall state the particulars of the land required to be hired, and the term for which the Council are authorized to hire the same, and that the Council are willing to treat for the hiring thereof. The Council shall in every such notice state a date consistent with the terms of the Order on which they require that the tenancy of the Council shall commence.

(2) Where the owner is a tenant the Council shall also give notice to the person in receipt of the rent reserved under the lease under which the owner holds as tenant that they require to hire compulsorily the lands specified in such notice.

(3) Where the land is authorized to be hired for the purpose of providing allotments or allotment gardens, the notices referred to in this Regulation must be served within three calendar months after the date of the Order or where confirmation of the Order is necessary, then after the date of the confirmation thereof.

7. On receipt of the particulars of the interest of an existing tenant, the Council shall within twenty-one days give notice to the tenant, stating whether the Council desire to extinguish the interest of such tenant or to hire the land subject to such interest, and if the Council fail to give such notice they shall be deemed to desire to extinguish the interest of the tenant. Any interest of an existing tenant which is extinguished under the powers conferred by a Compulsory Order shall be extinguished upon, and by reason of, the commencement of the tenancy of the Council.

8.—(1) An existing tenant whose interest in the land is extinguished upon, and by reason of, the commencement of the tenancy of the Council shall be entitled to recover from the Council compensation for the value of his interest in the land and for any just allowance which ought to be made to him by an incoming tenant, and for any loss or injury which the existing tenant may sustain.

(2) If any person claim compensation in respect of any unexpired term or interest under any lease of lands by the Order authorized to be hired, the Council may require such person to produce the lease in respect of which such claim is made, or sufficient evidence thereof, and if, after demand made in writing by the Council, such lease, or such evidence thereof, be not produced within twenty-one days, the party so claiming compensation shall be considered as a tenant holding only from year to year, and be entitled to compensation accordingly.

9. If the owner of land authorized by a Compulsory Order to be hired is unable, except under powers conferred by these Regulations, to lease the land for the term and on the conditions for and on which the Council are so authorized to hire the land, the rent to be paid by the Council shall be determined, as in default of agreement, under and in accordance with the provisions of the Acquisition of Land (Assessment of Compensation) Act, 1919, and the Small Holdings and Allotments Acts, 1908 to 1919, and the Allotments Act, 1922.

10. If an existing tenant is unable, except under powers conferred by these Regulations, to dispose of the interest created by the lease under which he holds and to give an absolute discharge for the compensation for such interest, the amount payable by the Council to the existing tenant or any person claiming through him in respect of such interest or in respect of improvements executed on the land or otherwise, and, where part only of the holding is hired the rent to be paid for the residue of the holding during the remainder of the term for which the holding is held, shall be determined, as in default of agreement, in manner provided by the preceding Regulation.

11. If the Council cannot after diligent inquiry ascertain the owner or existing tenant, or if for twenty-one days after the giving of such notice to treat to the owner or existing tenant as is required by these Regulations, he fail to state the particulars demanded by the notice or fail to treat with the Council in respect of his interest, or if the owner or the existing tenant do not agree with the Council as to any matter which under paragraph (3) of Part II of the First Schedule to the Act of 1908 is in default of such agreement to be determined as therein provided, the Council may require that the rent, compensation or other matter to be determined shall be determined in manner provided by the Acquisition of Land (Assessment of Compensation) Act, 1919, and the Small Holdings and Allotments Acts, 1908 to 1919, and the Allotments Act, 1922.

12. If the land authorized to be compulsorily hired is held by the owner subject to any reservation or exception or easement from which the Council require that the land when leased to the Council shall be exonerated during the existence of the lease, any person injuriously affected by the exoneration of the land from such reservation or exception or by the extinguishment of the easement effected by the lease to the Council shall be entitled to recover compensation for the injury from the Council, and the amount of the compensation shall in default of agreement between such person and the Council be determined under and in accordance with the provisions of the Acquisition of Land (Assess-

ment of Compensation) Act, 1919, and the Small Holdings and Allotments Acts, 1908 to 1919, and the Allotments Act, 1922.

13. In determining the rent to be paid by the Council for land authorized to be compulsorily hired the interest of any existing tenant and the existence of any reservation or exception or easement affecting the land shall be taken into consideration, and the land shall be valued as subject to such interest, reservation, exception, or easement.

14.—(1) In determining the rent to be paid for land authorized to be compulsorily hired regard shall be had by the arbitrator not only to the value of the land to be hired, but also to the damage (if any) to be sustained by the owner of the land by reason of its severance from other land of such owner, or by reason of such other land being otherwise injuriously affected by the exercise of the powers conferred on the Council by the Compulsory Order, the Small Holdings and Allotments Acts, 1908 to 1919, or by the Allotments Act, 1922.

(2) Every existing tenant shall be entitled to receive from the Council compensation for the damage done to him in his tenancy by reason of the severance of the land to be hired from land which is held by such tenant and is not required to be hired.

15.—(1) If the land authorized to be compulsorily hired is land of copyhold or customary tenure which cannot be leased by the owner for such a lease as is authorized by the Compulsory Order except with a licence of the lord of the manor of which the land is held, and the owner shall not obtain such licence before the execution of the lease, this shall be taken into consideration in determining the rent payable by the Council, and the lord of the manor shall be entitled to recover compensation from the Council for any loss sustained by reason of the lease being under these Regulations made valid and effectual without a licence, and the amount of the compensation shall in default of agreement between the lord and the Council be determined under and in accordance with the provisions of the Acquisition of Land (Assessment of Compensation) Act, 1919, and the Small Holdings and Allotments Acts, 1908 to 1919, and the Allotments Act, 1922.

(2) Every such lease shall be entered on the rolls of the manor in every case in which by the custom of the manor such a lease granted with the licence of the lord is required to be so entered; and the steward of the manor shall cause such lease to be so entered, and shall give to the Council a certificate of such entry on payment to such steward of the accustomed fees, or, if there be no accustomed fees, on payment of such sum as may in default of agreement be adjudged by a Court of Summary Jurisdiction, on the application of such steward or the Council, to be payable in respect of such entry.

16.—(1) As soon as the amount of the rent to be paid by the Council for the land proposed to be compulsorily hired, and the amount of any other compensation to be paid by the Council to any person entitled thereto in respect of the land or any interest therein, or in respect of improvements executed on the land or otherwise, have been determined, so far as the same can be determined before the tenancy of the Council commences, the owner shall on the application of the Council execute a lease of the land in accordance with the Order, subject only to the interest of any existing tenant which the Council have given notice that they do not desire to extinguish, and to any reservation, exception or easement subject to which the land is to be hired, and if the owner refuses or after notice in writing by the Council fails within one month, to execute the lease, or if the owner of the land cannot after diligent inquiry be ascertained by the Council, the Council shall execute the lease in duplicate, and shall forward one copy to the owner, if he can be found, and a lease so executed shall take effect as if it had been duly executed by the owner.

(2) A lease executed by the owner, or by the Council under this Regulation, shall be binding on and enure for the benefit of all persons interested in the land hired, and shall not cause any forfeiture of the land, or of any land held therewith or create any right of entry on any such land, or any right of action for breach of a covenant not to assign, or like covenant.

17. The lease to the Council shall, when executed in accordance with these Regulations, and subject as hereinafter provided, take effect as from the date specified by the Council in the notice to treat given by the Council to the owner of the land, and in such case the Council shall on the date so specified be entitled to enter on the land, subject to the interest of any existing tenant which is not to be extinguished by the hiring ;

Provided that this Regulation is subject to the power of the Council under subsection (8) of section 39 of the Act of 1908 to withdraw such notice to treat.

18.—(1) Costs reasonably incurred by the owner in connection with the preparation and execution of the lease and any counterpart and costs reasonably incurred by the owner or an existing tenant in furnishing any particulars of his estate and interest required by notice under these Regulations, or otherwise required by the Council, shall be paid by the Council to the owner or tenant as the case may be.

(2) If the Council and the party entitled to any such costs do not agree as to the amount thereof, such costs shall be taxed by one of the Taxing Masters of the High Court, upon an Order of the Court to be obtained upon petition in a summary way by either of the parties ; and the Council shall pay what the said Master shall certify to be due in respect of such costs to the party entitled thereto, or in default thereof the same may be recovered in the same way as any other costs payable under an Order of the Court, and the expense of taxing such costs shall be borne by the Council unless upon such taxation one-sixth part of the amount of such costs be disallowed, in which case the costs of such taxation shall be borne by the party whose costs shall be so taxed, and the amount thereof shall be ascertained by the said Master, and deducted by him accordingly in his certificate of such taxation.

19. If in any case the Council are authorized by a Compulsory Order and these Regulations to enter upon and hold any land authorized to be compulsorily hired, and the owner or occupier of any such lands or any other person refuses to give up the possession thereof, or hinders the Council from entering upon

the same, a court of summary jurisdiction, on complaint made by the Council, may require the owner or occupier of such land or other person to deliver possession of the same to the Council or permit them to enter thereon ; and any Order made under these provisions may be enforced as provided by section 34 of the Summary Jurisdiction Act, 1879.

20. The arbitrator shall within one month after his appointment, or within such extended time as the Minister shall allow, make and sign a determination of all matters referred to him for determination which are in his opinion capable of being ascertained at the date of the determination, and shall within one month after the commencement of the tenancy of the Council, or within such extended time as the Minister shall allow, make and sign a determination of all matters referred to him for determination which are not determined by the previous determination.

21. Every determination made by an arbitrator shall be duly stamped by him and sent as soon as possible to the Council and a copy shall at the same time be sent to the owner and any existing tenant affected by the determination.

22.—(1) Any compensation, other than rent, payable by the Council in respect of the compulsory hiring, including any compensation payable in respect of the interest of an existing tenant which is extinguished by such hiring, shall be payable by the Council in manner provided by these Regulations on the execution of the lease, or if payable in respect of any matter not then determined, on the date when it is duly determined.

(2) Subject to any provision in the Compulsory Order and these Regulations, compensation so payable by the Council shall be paid on demand to the owner, or the existing tenant, as the case may be.

23. Subject to any provision in the Compulsory Order relating to mines and minerals, there shall, unless the owner and the Council otherwise agree, be excepted and reserved out of the lease all the mines and minerals, metals, ores, and other substrata, whether of coal, stone, clay, sand, or any other metalliferous or mineral substance or produce whatsoever, whether opened or unopened, worked or unworked, within or under the hired land (all which are hereinafter collectively referred to as " the said mines and minerals ") ; with full liberty and power for the persons entitled to the said mines and minerals at all times during the lease by underground workings only to win, work, and carry away the whole of the said mines and minerals, and also to carry away the produce of any other mines ; nevertheless making reasonable compensation for any damage or subsidence which may be occasioned to any building on the land hired by reason of such working and carrying away of the said mines and minerals as aforesaid or the exercise of the powers to be reserved as aforesaid, such compensation to be settled in case of dispute by a single arbitrator in accordance with the Agricultural Holdings Act, 1908.

24. Except as in these Regulations expressly provided, any person interested in the determination of any matter under these Regulations shall not be required to produce to the person making the valuation, or give him access to, any document of title.

## Part III.
### General.

25.—(1) Every notice required to be given by a Council to an owner, existing tenant, or other person interested in land proposed or authorized to be hired, shall either be served personally on such person or sent by post to or left at his usual place of abode in the United Kingdom, if any such can after diligent inquiry be found, and in case any such person shall be absent from the United Kingdom or cannot be found after diligent inquiry, shall be sent by post to or left with any agent ordinarily receiving the rents of the land on behalf of such person, and a copy thereof shall also be sent by post to or left with the occupier of the land to which such notice relates, or, if there be no such occupier, shall be affixed upon some conspicuous part of such land.

(2) If an owner, existing tenant, or other person interested be a Corporation aggregate such notice shall be sent by post to or left at the principal office of business of such Corporation, or if no such office can after diligent inquiry be found, shall be sent by post to or served on some principal officer, if any, of such corporation.

26.—(1) Section two of the Land Settlement (Facilities) Act, 1919 (*Power of entry on land*), shall apply in the case of an Order authorizing the compulsory hiring of land, or of an agreement to hire land, subject to the following adaptations :—

(a) " Hire " or " hiring " shall, as the context requires, be substituted for " purchase " ;

(b) A notice under Regulation 6 of these Regulations shall be deemed to be a notice to treat.

(2) In the case of an Order for the compulsory hiring of land and entry by a Council on the land or any part thereof under sub-section (1) of the said section as adapted by this regulation the compensation payable in respect of the hiring of the land shall include such compensation by way of rent or otherwise, together with interest on such part of the compensation as is not paid by way of rent at the rate of five per cent. per annum from the time of entry on the land until such compensation is paid, as would have been payable if the Council had at the date of entry hired the land of which possession is taken and extinguished the interest therein of any existing tenant.

27. Where under the Acquisition of Land (Assessment of Compensation) Act, 1919, any matter to which these Regulations relate is determined by the Commissioners of Inland Revenue, any provision in these Regulations referring to an arbitrator shall subject to the necessary modifications apply to the Commissioners.

28. In these Regulations, unless the context otherwise requires—

" Minister " means the Minister of Agriculture and Fisheries ;

" Owner " in relation to any land proposed or authorized to be hired means the person who by himself or his agent is in actual possession, or receipt of the rents and profits of the land (except a tenant thereof under a lease for a term no greater than the term for which the land is proposed or authorized to be hired) and that without regard to the real amount of interest of such person ;

"Existing tenant" in relation to any land proposed or authorized to be hired means a tenant thereof under a lease for a term no greater than the term for which the land is proposed or authorized to be hired ;

"Lease" includes an agreement for a lease ;

"Compulsory Order" means an Order under the Acts of 1908 to 1919 and the Act of 1922 which authorize land to be compulsorily hired ;

"Land" includes stints and other alienable common rights of grazing.

29. A Compulsory Order shall incorporate these Regulations, but shall not, unless therein otherwise expressly stated, incorporate any of the provisions of the Lands Clauses Acts or of sections 77 to 85 of the Railway Clauses Act, 1845, except so far as such provisions have been incorporated with adaptations in these Regulations.

30. These Regulations shall apply to a compulsory hiring by the Small Holdings Commissioners acting in default of a Council or by the Minister, with the substitution of those Commissioners or the Minister, as the case may be, for the Council.

31. The Compulsory Order and these Regulations shall not extend and apply to—

Any land belonging to His Majesty the King, his heirs and successors in right of the Crown, or in right of the Duchy of Lancaster ; nor to

Any land belonging to the Duchy of Cornwall ; nor to

Any land subject to rights of common.

32. The Small Holdings and Allotments (Compulsory Hiring) Regulations, 1919, are hereby revoked but not so as to affect the operation of any Order made before the date of these Regulations.

33. These Regulations may be cited as the Small Holdings and Allotments (Compulsory Hiring) Regulations, 1922.

In witness whereof the Official Seal of the Minister of Agriculture and Fisheries is hereunto affixed this twenty-sixth day of September, nineteen hundred and twenty-two.

(L.S.) H. L. FRENCH,
*Assistant Secretary.*

## APPENDIX.

### *Form of Order for Compulsory Hiring.*

1. The \*     are hereby empowered to put in force as respects the land described in the draft lease set forth in the schedule hereto the powers of

---

\* Insert "County Council of            ," or "County Council of            acting on behalf of the Parish Council" [*or* "Meeting"] or "Mayor, Aldermen, and Burgesses of the Borough of            ," or "District Council."

compulsory hiring conferred by the Small Holdings and Allotments Acts, 1908 to 1919,† subject to the provisions of those Acts and to the Small Holdings and Allotments (Compulsory Hiring) Regulations, 1922, and to the terms of this Order.

2. The tenancy of the Council shall commence either on the [*twenty-fifth day of March*] or the [*twenty-ninth day of September*].‡

3. (*Where the land is glebe land or other land belonging to an ecclesiastical benefice insert the following paragraph.*) Any sum payable by way of compensation for the damage to be sustained by the owner by reason of severance or other injury affecting the land shall not be paid as directed by the Lands Clauses Acts, but shall be paid to the Ecclesiastical Commissioners to be applied by them as money paid to them upon a sale under the Ecclesiastical Leasing Acts of land belonging to a benefice.

4. (*Where the Order relates to small holdings insert the following paragraph.*) The powers conferred by this Order shall cease after the expiration of one year from the date of confirmation of this Order by the Minister of Agriculture and Fisheries, unless such period is extended by the Minister.

5. (*Where the Order relates to allotments or allotment gardens insert the following paragraph.*) The powers conferred by this Order shall cease after the expiration of three calendar months from the date hereof or from the date of confirmation by the Minister of Agriculture and Fisheries if the Order is so confirmed.

*Schedule to Form of Order for Compulsory Hiring.*

This Schedule shall contain a draft of the lease under which it is proposed that the land shall be authorized to be acquired by the Council, setting out all the proposed terms and conditions except the date of the commencement of the tenancy and the rent.

The lease shall contain covenants by the Council to cultivate the land in a proper manner and to pay to the landlord at the determination of the tenancy, on the Council quitting the land, compensation for any depreciation of the land by reason of any failure by the Council, or any person deriving title under them, to observe such covenants, or by reason of any user of the land by the Council or such person as aforesaid, and, unless otherwise agreed, a covenant by the Council to keep the buildings and premises demised in repair.

The lease shall not authorize the breaking up of pasture unless the Council are prepared to prove to the satisfaction of the Minister of Agriculture and Fisheries that it can be so broken up without depreciating the value of the land, or that the circumstances are such that small holdings [allotments] cannot otherwise be successfully cultivated.

---

† Insert here " and the Allotments Act, 1922," if the Order is made for the purpose of providing allotments or allotment gardens.

‡ These dates shall be the half-yearly days customary in the district, but where the Order is made for the purpose of providing allotment gardens, the date of the commencement of the Council's tenancy shall not be a date between the 6th day of April and the 29th day of September.

If the Order relates to the provision of land for allotment gardens, the lease should so state, and the foregoing paragraph relating to the breaking up of pasture is not applicable.

If the land authorized to be acquired for allotment gardens is the property of a corporation or company acquired by them for the purposes of a railway, dock, canal, water or other public undertaking, the lease shall contain a condition enabling the corporation or company to resume possession of the land when required by them for the purpose (not being the use of land for agriculture) for which it was acquired by the corporation or company.

The lease shall also provide that, except with the consent of the landlord, the Council shall not fell or cut timber or trees, or take, sell, or carry away any minerals, gravel, sand, or clay, except so far as may be necessary or convenient for the purpose of erecting buildings on the land or otherwise adapting the land for small holdings [allotments] [allotment gardens], and except upon payment of compensation for minerals, gravel, sand, or clay so used.

The lease shall also provide that any question as to the amount of compensation payable by the Council under the lease shall be determined where the land is authorized to be acquired for small holdings by a single arbitrator in accordance with the Agricultural Holdings Act, 1908, and where the land is authorized to be acquired for allotments or allotment gardens in manner provided by the Allotments Act, 1922.

(VIII)

**MODEL RULES AS TO ALLOTMENT GARDENS ISSUED BY THE MINISTRY OF AGRICULTURE AND FISHERIES.**

The making of Rules by a Borough District or Parish Council under section 28 of the Small Holdings and Allotments Act, 1908, is optional. Such Rules require to be confirmed by the Minister of Agriculture and Fisheries before they can be of any force.

Any Council proposing to make Rules should submit a draft copy to the Ministry ; a copy of the Model Rules can be used for this purpose. Where it is proposed to make alterations of any importance it may save time and correspondence if the circumstances are explained when the draft is submitted.

ALLOTMENTS ACTS, 1908 TO 1922.

ALLOTMENT RULES.

Made by the *
with respect to allotment gardens for the †

---

\* Insert " Mayor, Aldermen and Burgesses of the Borough of acting by the Council " or " Urban District Council of ," or " Parish Council of ."
† Insert " said Borough " or " said Urban District," or " Parish of ."

# MODEL RULES 135

*Interpretation of Terms.*

1. Throughout these Rules the expression "the Council" means the *
and includes any committee of the Council or any allotment managers appointed by the Council under the Allotments Acts, 1908 to 1922.

*Definition of the persons eligible to be tenants of the Allotment Gardens.*

2. Any man or woman who at the time of application to the Council for an allotment is resident in the †
shall be eligible to become a tenant of an allotment garden, subject to the statutory provision that one person shall not hold allotments acquired under the above-mentioned Acts exceeding five acres.

*Division of the land into Allotment Gardens.*

3. The Council, before giving notice of their intention to let any land for allotment gardens, shall divide the land, and shall cause a plan to be prepared showing each allotment garden, and distinguishing it by a separate number.

*Notices to be given for the letting of the Allotment Gardens.*

4. The Council shall give public notice by bills or placards posted in some conspicuous places in the †          or otherwise exhibited therein, setting forth the particulars as to any allotment garden which they propose to let.

Such notice shall specify the allotment gardens to be let, the rent to be paid for the same, the name and address of the Clerk to the Council to whom applications for the hiring of an allotment garden are to be sent, and the last day for receiving applications.

If any special condition is to apply to the allotment gardens, or any of them, the notice shall specify such condition, or state where copies of the Form of Agreement for Letting of such allotment gardens may be seen.

If the tenant is to pay for tenant right or compensation for improvements this fact and the amount if then ascertained shall be stated in the notice.

*Rules as to the letting of the Allotment Gardens, and for preventing any undue preference in the letting thereof.*

5. The Council shall not let any allotment garden unless and until notice that they propose to let the same has been duly given in pursuance of the Rule in that behalf at least two weeks before the last day for receiving an application for such allotment garden.

Every application for an allotment garden shall be in the

---

\* Insert "Mayor, Aldermen and Burgesses of the Borough of          acting by the Council" or "Urban District Council of          ," or "Parish Council of          ."
† Insert "Borough" or "District" or "Parish."

K

Form appended to these Rules or to the like effect, and shall be sent or delivered to the Clerk to the Council.

In letting an allotment garden for which there are two or more applicants eligible to become tenants and likely to keep the allotment garden in a proper state of cultivation, preference shall be given to an applicant who does not hold an allotment or agricultural land (other than a garden of 20 poles or less attached to his residence) either from the Council or otherwise over an applicant who does hold such land, but subject to such preference the tenant shall be determined by the drawing of lots by the Council. A quitting tenant of land shall for the purposes of this Rule be treated as not holding that land.

### *Agreements for letting Allotment Gardens.*

6. An agreement to let an allotment garden to an applicant may be signed by the Clerk to the Council on behalf of the Council, and may be in the Form set out in the Schedule to these Rules.

### *General Conditions under which the Allotment Gardens are to be cultivated.*

7. The tenant of an allotment garden shall comply with the following conditions :—
   (1) He shall keep the allotment garden clean and in good state of cultivation and fertility and in good condition.
   (2) He shall not cause any nuisance or annoyance to the occupier of any other allotment garden or obstruct any path set out by the Council for the use of the occupiers of the allotment gardens.
   (3) He shall not underlet, assign, or part with the possession of the allotment garden or any part of it, without the written consent of the Council.
   (4) He shall not without the written consent of the Council cut or prune any timber or other trees, or take, sell, or carry away any mineral, gravel, sand, or clay.
   (5) He shall keep every hedge that forms part of the allotment garden properly cut and trimmed, keep all ditches properly cleansed, and shall maintain and keep in repair any other fences and any gates on the allotment garden.
   (6) He shall not without the written consent of the Council erect any building on the allotment garden.
   (7) He shall not use barbed wire for a fence adjoining any path set out by the council for the use of the occupiers of the allotment gardens.
   (8) He shall, as regards the allotment garden, observe and perform all conditions and covenants contained in the lease (if any), under which the Council hold the land.
   (9) He shall observe and perform any other special condition which the Council consider necessary to preserve the allotment garden from deterioration, and of which notice to applicants for the allotment garden is given in accordance with these Rules.

## MODEL RULES

### Payment of Rent.

8. The rent of an allotment garden shall, unless otherwise agreed in writing, be paid half-yearly on the (*insert dates*) in each year.

### Power to inspect Allotment Gardens.

9. Any member or officer of the Council shall be entitled at any time when directed by the Council to enter and inspect an allotment garden.

### Termination of a tenancy of an Allotment Garden.

10. The tenancy of an allotment garden shall, unless otherwise agreed in writing, terminate on the half-yearly rent day next after the death of the tenant, and shall also terminate whenever the tenancy or right of occupation of the Council terminates.

It may also be terminated by the Council by re-entry after one month's notice—
   (1) if the rent is in arrear for not less than 40 days; or
   (2) if the tenant is not duly observing the Rules affecting the allotment garden, or any other term or condition of his tenancy, or if the tenant becomes bankrupt or compounds with his creditors.

The tenancy may also be terminated by the Council or tenant by six months' notice in writing, expiring on *

### Exemption of certain Lettings from these Rules.

11. These Rules shall not apply to any land let to an Association, or to any allotment garden which the Council, under special circumstances to be recorded in their minutes, may exempt from these Rules, but shall apply, except as aforesaid, to an allotment garden though held under a tenancy made before these Rules come into operation, but not so as to affect any right to compensation for an improvement executed before these Rules come into operation.

### Service of Notices.

12. Any notice may be served on a tenant either personally or by leaving it at his last-known place of abode or by registered letter addressed to him there, or by fixing the same in some conspicuous manner on the allotment garden.

#### FORM OF APPLICATION FOR ALLOTMENT GARDENS.

To the Clerk to the †
I the undersigned hereby make application for one [*or* No.
] of the allotment gardens provided by the Council at—
1. Name.
2. Residence.
3. Age.

---

* This date must be on or before the 6th April or on or after the 29th September.

† Insert " Town Council for the Borough of ," or " Urban District Council of ," or " Parish Council of ."

4. How long resident in the *
5. Whether holding any allotment, or agricultural land (other than a garden of 20 poles or less attached to my residence), and if so—
    (a) From whom
    (b) Extent of land so held
    (c) Whether quitting the land, and if so when

In the event of my application being granted, I agree when required by the Council to sign an agreement for letting in accordance with the Rules, and to pay the stamp duty (if any) on such agreement,† and to pay for tenant right and compensation for improvements the sum stated in the Notice of Letting (*or such sum as shall be found due to the outgoing tenant for such matters*).

Signature
Date

## SCHEDULE.

### Form of Agreement for Letting.

Agreement made this      day of      19   , between the ‡      (herein-after called the Council) of the one part, and      of      (herein-after called the tenant) of the other part, whereby the Council agrees to let, and the tenant agrees to hire as a yearly tenant from the day of      19   , the allotment garden[s] numbered      in the register of allotment gardens provided by the Council and containing      or thereabouts [§ subject to the exceptions and reservations contained in the lease under which the Council hold the land] at the yearly rent of
payable half-yearly and at a proportionate rent for any part of a year over which the tenancy may extend.

The tenancy is subject to the Allotment Rules made from time to time by the Council and to the Allotments Acts, 1908 to 1922.

Rates in respect of the allotment garden shall be paid by the ‖

                Signed
                         Clerk to the Council

Witness

                Signed
                         Tenant.

Witness

[*Any special conditions affecting the allotment garden are to be endorsed on the agreement.*]

---

\* Insert " Borough," " District " or " Parish."
† Stamp duty will not be payable if the rent does not exceed 10s. per annum and no premium is paid.
‡ Insert " Town Council for the Borough of      ," or " Urban District Council of      ," or " Parish Council of      ."
§ Omit words in brackets if inapplicable.
‖ Insert " Council " or " tenant " as the case may be.

## (IX)

## RULES WHICH MUST BE ADOPTED BY ANY ASSOCIATION OR SOCIETY DESIRING TO PURCHASE OR HIRE LAND FROM A LOCAL AUTHORITY UNDER THE SMALL HOLDINGS AND ALLOTMENTS ACTS, 1908 to 1919, AND THE ALLOTMENTS ACT, 1922.

### SMALL HOLDINGS AND ALLOTMENTS.

The objects of the Society shall include the business of creating or promoting the creation of small holdings or allotments, and encouraging their proper cultivation, with power to acquire land from local authorities acting under the provisions of any Act for the time being in force relating to small holdings or allotments, or from any other person or body ; to adapt any land so acquired for small holdings or allotments, to acquire or erect dwelling-houses or other buildings, or to execute any other improvement, and to let the land, houses, and buildings to members of the Society.

### *Small Holdings and Allotments Separate Account.*

A separate account shall be kept by the Society of all receipts and expenditure of the Society under the rule headed " Small Holdings and Allotments." The receipts shall be applicable for the following purposes and for no other purpose whether during the existence of the Society or on dissolution :—
(1) For payment of the expenses of managing land, houses, and buildings acquired or erected under the said Rule, including payment of rent, rates, taxes, and other like outgoings.
(2) For payment of expenses of repairs or improvements from time to time made by the Society on such land, houses, and buildings.
(3) For payment to the general account of the Society of interest at the rate of £5 per cent per annum on all capital expenditure by the Society on the acquisition or adaptation of such land, houses, and buildings.
(4) For recouping capital expenditure by the Society on improvement or adaptation of the land, houses, and buildings within such period as is reasonable having regard to the probable duration of the improvement or work of adaptation.
(5) For forming a Special Reserve Fund not exceeding one year's annual value of the land, houses, and buildings, and so that such reserve fund shall be available for any purpose authorized by this Rule but for no other purpose.
(6) For prizes for the encouragement of the proper cultivation of the land ; and
(7) For the benefit of the tenants generally, in such manner as the Committee may determine.

Nothing in this rule shall be deemed to prohibit an arrangement between the Society and a tenant for the repayment or

# APPENDIX

rebatement of part of the rent payable by him to the society. Nothing in this rule shall prejudice or affect any right or remedy of any creditor of the Society.

## (X)

### SCHEDULE OF TERMS

which the Ministry of Health will Allow for the Repayment of Loans for Adaptation of Allotments.

DESCRIPTION OF WORK.

*Fencing.*

|   | TERM YEARS. |
|---|---|
| Ordinary deal | 8 |
| Ordinary larch | 12 |
| Larch rails and oak posts | 25 |
| Deal and larch— | |
|   (a) If treated with a preservative under pressure | 20 |
|   (b) If treated by hot steeping | 15 |
| Oak posts and rails | 25 |
| Chestnut piles with galvanized wire and stiffening posts | 12 to 15 |
| Posts of re-inforced concrete | 20 |
| Continuous bar iron (substantial) | 25 to 30 |
| Stranded wire with steel, wrought iron, or oak standards and straining posts | 25 |
| Ditto, with wooden posts, other than oak, the posts being treated with a preservative— | |
|   (a) Under pressure | 20 |
|   (b) By hot steeping | 15 |
| Welded wire with creosoted posts | 15 |
| Ditto, with iron posts | 20 |
| Woven wire fencing, welded | 10 |
| Ditto, not welded | 5 |
| Stone walling, dry with proper coping | 25 |
| Ditto, in mortar, depending on nature of stone | 30 to 40 |

*Water Supply.*

| | |
|---|---|
| Cast-iron pipes not exceeding 1-inch in diameter | 20 |
| Ditto, over 1-inch in diameter | 30 |
| Steel tubes not exceeding 1-inch in diameter | 15 |
| Ditto, over 1-inch in diameter | 20 |
| Wells | 30 |
| Ditto, dug and brick lined | 50 |
| Ditto, lined with reinforced concrete | 20 |
| Ditto, tube with pump | 25 |

*Roads.*

| | |
|---|---|
| Bush and burnt ballast | 5 |
| Stone, gravel, slag, or clinker, with good foundations and drainage | 25 |

# INDEX

|  | PAGE |
|---|---|
| Accounts of Councils— | |
| Annual statement of receipts and expenditure | 37 |
| Acquisition of Land (Assessment of Compensation) Act, 1919 | 107 |
| Acquisition of Land— | |
| By agreement | 14 |
| By compulsion | 15 |
| By county councils | 11 |
| For common pasture | 10 |
| For fee farm and other rents | 14 |
| For whom it may be acquired | 5 |
| Restrictions on | 15 |
| Adaptation— | |
| Drainage, fencing, etc. | 7 |
| Erection of houses | 9 |
| Admiralty land | 39 |
| Agreement for letting | 138 |
| Agricultural Holdings Act, 1908 | 38, 46, 47 |
| Agricultural Organization Society | 12 |
| Agricultural Land Sales (Restriction of Notices to Quit) Act 1919 | 56 |
| Agriculture Act, 1920 | 44, 51, 114 |
| Air Council land | 39 |
| Allotments Act, 1922 | 93 |
| Applications, to whom to be made | 3 |
| Appropriation of land, council's powers | 8 |
| Arbitration— | |
| As to good faith of owner desiring to resume possession of land | 41 |
| Compensation on withdrawal of notice to treat | 30 |
| Compulsory acquisition | 27 |
| Arbitrator, Appointment of | 27 |
| Ascertaining demand | 7 |
| Associations | 12 |
| | |
| Borough Council— | |
| Accounts | 37 |
| Acquisition of land | 14 |
| Allotment Committees | 3–5 |
| Allotment Managers | 5 |
| Borrowing powers | 34 |
| Default of | 11 |
| Duty to provide allotments or allotment gardens | 3 |
| Expenses | 35 |

## INDEX

|  | PAGE |
|---|---|
| Interchange of land for small holdings | 9 |
| Limitation on fresh expenditure | 35 |
| Model Rules | 134 |
| Sale and hire of fruit-trees, seeds, implements, etc. | 9 |
| Borrowing powers of councils | 34 |
| Building, Land let required for | 38 |
| Building value not to be considered on compulsory hiring | 17, 29 |

Canal company—
| Compulsory hiring of land owned by | 16 |
| Power of re-entry on land let | 39 |
| Commissioners Small, Holdings | 11 |
| Committees | 3 |
| Common pasture, Provision of | 10 |
| Commons and open spaces | 16 |

Compensation—
| On occasion of compulsory purchase or hiring | 27 |
| On withdrawal of notice to treat (compulsory acquisition) | 30 |
| Under Acquisition of Land (Assessment of Compensation) Act, 1919 | 27 |

Compensation to allotment tenants—
| Assessment and recovery of | 48 |
| Basis, etc. | 44, 46 |
| Mortgagee, Liability for | 47 |
| Table of | 50 |

Compulsory acquisition of land—
| General | 15 |
| Hiring | 18 |
| Order for hiring | 18 |
| Order for purchase | 123 |
| Powers of councils | 15 |
| Procedure for | 17 |
| Purchase | 18 |
| Regulations, hiring | 124 |
| Regulations purchase | 120 |
| Restrictions on | 15 |
| Terms of hiring | 18, 19 |
| Unconditional offer | 27 |
| Conditions of letting | 134 |

Co-operative Associations or Societies—
| Grants to | 34 |
| Rules | 139 |
| Sale and letting to | 12 |
| Co-opted members of committees | 4 |
| Cottage gardens | 1, 2 |
| County boroughs, special provisions | 8 |
| County Councils, Powers and duties | 10 |
| County Court Judge, Appointment of valuer by | 48 |
| Crops, damage to by trespass, etc. | 56 |
| Crown lands | 56 |
| Cultivation | 6 |

# INDEX

| | PAGE |
|---|---|
| Damage to allotment gardens, penalty | 56 |

Definitions—
  Agriculture . . . . . . . . 40
  Allotment . . . . . . . . 1
  Allotment garden . . . . . . . 2
  Association . . . . . . . . 13
  Cultivation . . . . . . . . 6
  Home Farm . . . . . . . . 17
  Industrial purpose . . . . . . . 40
  Landlord . . . . . . . . 48
  Owner . . . . . . . . . 32
  Unoccupied land . . . . . . . 31
Demand for—
  How ascertained . . . . . . . 7
  How to be satisfied . . . . . . 3
Determination of tenancies . . . . . . 38
Dock Company—
  Compulsory hiring of land owned by . . . 16
  Power of re-entry on land let . . . . 39
Drainage . . . . . . . . . 7
Dwelling-houses . . . . . . . . 9

Enter, Power to, for purpose of inspection . . . 86
Entry, Power of, acquisition of land . . . . 31
Expenditure of councils—
  General . . . . . . . . 35
  Separate accounts to be kept . . . . 37
Expiration of tenancies—
  Compensation . . . . . . . 44
  Councils' right to compensation . . . . 49
  Tenant's right to remove trees, bushes, etc. . . 43

Fees, official arbitrator . . . . . . . 28
Fencing . . . . . . . . . 140
Fertilizers, purchase of, by Councils . . . . 9
Finance . . . . . . . . . 34
Fixtures, removal of . . . . . . . 43
Forms—
  Agreement for letting . . . . . . 138
  Applications . . . . . . . . 137
  Lease to Council . . . . . . . 19
  Notice of entry (compulsory acquisition) . . 26
  Notice of order . . . . . . . 22, 23
  Notice to treat . . . . . . . 24
  Order for compulsory hiring . . . . . 18
  Order for compulsory purchase . . . . 123
  Rules, model, for letting . . . . . 134
  Rules, model, co-operative associations . . 139
Fruit trees—
  Compensation for . . . . . . . 47
  Purchase of, by councils . . . . . 9
  Removal of . . . . . . . . 43
  Rules as to planting . . . . . . 47

|  | PAGE |
|---|---|
| General Rate Metropolis | 54 |
| General District Rates | 54 |
| Grazing rights, provision of | 10 |

Hiring—
|  |  |
|---|---|
| Of land by agreement | 14 |
| Of land by compulsion | 18 |
| Power to renew | 18 |
| Regulations for compulsory | 124 |
| Renewal of compulsory | 31 |
| Home farm, restriction on compulsory acquisition | 15 |

|  |  |
|---|---|
| Implements, purchase of by councils | 9 |

Improvements—
|  |  |
|---|---|
| Adaptation, etc. | 7 |
| Compensation for | 46 |

Land—
|  |  |
|---|---|
| Adaptation of | 7 |
| Compulsory acquisition of | 15 |
| Interchange for small holdings | 9 |
| Power to resume possession of | 38 |
| Voluntary acquisition of | 14 |
| Land Settlement (Facilities) Act, 1919 | 83 |
| Landlord, power of, to resume possession | 38 |
| Lease when land compulsorily hired | 19 |

Letting—
|  |  |
|---|---|
| Agreement for | 138 |
| Of superfluous land | 8 |
| Rules as to | 134 |
| Limitation on local authorities' expenditure | 35 |

Loans—
|  |  |
|---|---|
| Co-operative societies | 34 |
| Interest on | 35 |
| Periods | 35, 140 |
| Public Works Loan Commissioners | 34 |
| Local inquiries | 11, 23 |
| Local Allotment Authorities | 3 |
| London, authorities responsible | 3 |

|  |  |
|---|---|
| Managers of allotments | 5 |
| Mansion house, restrictions on acquisition of home farm attached to | 15 |
| Market garden improvements | 47 |
| Metropolitan boroughs | 2, 3 |
| Mining, Land let required for | 38 |

Ministry of Agriculture and Fisheries—
|  |  |
|---|---|
| Annual report | 77 |
| Chief authority except as to finance | 11 |
| Compulsory hiring regulations | 124 |
| Compulsory purchase regulations | 120 |
| Confirmation of compulsory orders | 21, 24 |
| Co-operative Associations, rules for | 139 |

# INDEX

|  | PAGE |
|---|---|
| Duties in default of councils | 11 |
| Model Rules | 134 |
| Transfer of powers to Small Holdings Commissioners | 11 |
| Ministry of Health | 4, 11, 34 |

| National Trust | 16, 32 |
|---|---|
| National Union of Allotment Holders | 12 |
| New Forest | 56 |

Notices—
| For letting | 135 |
|---|---|
| Of entry | 26 |
| Of order for compulsory hiring | 18 |
| Of order for compulsory purchase | 123 |
| To determine tenancy | 38, 40 |

Notice to treat—
| For compulsory hiring | 24 |
|---|---|
| Period within which they must be served | 25 |
| Withdrawal of | 30 |

| Official arbitrators | 27 |
|---|---|
| Open spaces and commons, Compulsory acquisition of | 16 |

Parish Councils—
| Accounts | 37 |
|---|---|
| Acquisition of land | 14, 15 |
| Allotment managers | 5 |
| Borrowing powers | 34 |
| Committees | 5 |
| County councils may acquire land to lease to | 11 |
| Default of | 11 |
| Duty to provide allotments | 3 |
| Expenses | 34 |
| Includes parish meeting | 10 |
| Interchange of land for small holdings | 9 |
| Model Rules | 134 |
| Sale and hire of fruit-trees, seeds, plants, fertilizers, and implements | 9 |

| Parish Meeting, included in references to parish council | 10 |
|---|---|
| Pasture land, Compulsory hiring of | 16 |
| Plants, purchase of by councils | 9 |
| Poor rate | 52 |
| Possession, recovery of by councils | 43 |

Procedure—
| For compulsory acquisition | 17 |
|---|---|
| Public Works Loan Commissioners | 34 |

Purchase of land—
| By agreement | 14 |
|---|---|
| By compulsion | 18 |

Railway Company—
| Compulsory hiring of land owned by | 16 |
|---|---|
| Power of re-entry on land let | 39 |

# INDEX

| | PAGE |
|---|---|
| Rating | 52 |
| Re-entry by landlord or owner on land let | 38 |

Regulations—
| | |
|---|---|
| Compulsory hiring | 124 |
| Compulsory purchase | 120 |
| For letting | 134 |

| | |
|---|---|
| Removal of fruit-trees, bushes, etc., by tenants | 43 |
| Renewal of tenancy where land is hired compulsorily | 18 |

Rent—
| | |
|---|---|
| In advance | 6 |
| In arrear | 37 |
| Of land compulsorily hired | 27 |
| On renewal of tenancy (compulsorily) | 31 |
| Recovery of | 37 |
| Statutory direction as to | 6 |

Reports—
| | |
|---|---|
| Annual, by Ministry to Parliament | 77 |
| Annual, by councils to Ministry | 77 |

| | |
|---|---|
| Representation by ratepayers or electors as to demand | 7 |
| Representative members of committees | 4 |
| Requirements of allotment holders, purchase by council for re-sale or hire | 9 |

Resumption of land—
| | |
|---|---|
| By landlord for building, etc. | 38 |
| Compulsorily hired | 30 |
| When rent is in arrear or for breach of conditions | 39 |
| When temporarily let | 8 |

| | |
|---|---|
| Royal Parks | 93 |

Rules—
| | |
|---|---|
| For letting allotments | 134 |
| For letting common pasture | 10 |
| For letting grazing rights | 10 |
| To be adopted by co-operative associations | 139 |

| | |
|---|---|
| Schoolrooms, use of | 10 |
| Seeds, purchase of by councils | 9 |
| Small Holdings and Allotments Act, 1908 | 59 |
| Small Holdings Commissioners | 11 |
| Stamp duty | 7 |
| Stints, provision of | 10 |
| Sub-letting | 6 |

Superfluous land—
| | |
|---|---|
| Interchange of, for small holdings | 9 |
| Sale or letting of | 9 |

| | |
|---|---|
| Table showing compensation which may be claimed by various classes of allotment holders | 50 |

Tenancy—
| | |
|---|---|
| Compensation on determination of | 44 |
| Conditions of | 138 |
| Determination of | 38 |
| Renewal of compulsory | 18 |

| | |
|---|---|
| Tenure | 38 |

# INDEX

|  | PAGE |
|---|---|
| Unsuitable land may be sold, let, or exchanged | 9 |

Urban District Councils—
| | |
|---|---|
| Accounts | 37 |
| Acquisition of land | 14 |
| Allotment managers | 5 |
| Borrowing powers | 34 |
| Committees | 3–5 |
| Default of | 11 |
| Duty to provide allotments or allotment gardens | 3 |
| Expenses | 34, 35 |
| Interchange of land for small holdings | 9 |
| Model Rules | 134 |
| Sale or hire of fruit-trees, seeds, plants, fertilizers or implements | 9 |

Valuation—
| | |
|---|---|
| Compensation | 48 |
| Compulsory acquisition | 29 |

| | |
|---|---|
| War Department land | 39 |

Water Company—
| | |
|---|---|
| Compulsory hiring of land owned by | 16 |
| Power of re-entry on land let | 39 |

Milton Keynes UK
Ingram Content Group UK Ltd.
UKHW041448070823
426454UK00001B/31